WORLDS BEYOND THOUGHT:

Conversations On Now-Consciousness

D1599795

BY THE SAME AUTHOR

NOW-CONSCIOUSNESS:
Exploring the World Beyond Thought

WORLDS BEYOND THOUGHT:

Conversations On Now-Consciousness

ALBERT BLACKBURN

IDYLWILD BOOKS   PUBLISHERS
Ojai, California

Published in 1988 by: IDYLWILD BOOKS
                        P.O. BOX 246
                        OJAI, CA 93023

Library of Congress Catalog Card Number: 87-82604

ISBN: 0-9613054-3-6

Cover Design: Ron Miller

Interior Design and Production: Expressions Unlimited

Manufactured in the United States of America

First Printing 1988

CONTENTS

                        *   *   *

Now-Consciousness Order Form
Further Exploration Into Now-Consciousness
  Tapes Order Form

A LITTLE FORETHOUGHT

ONE EVENING IN 1808, A DISTRAUGHT, NERVOUS MAN WALKED INTO THE OFFICES OF DR. JAMES HAMILTON IN MANCHESTER. STRUCK BY HIS ANGUISHED LOOK, THE DOCTOR ASKED, "ARE YOU SICK?"

"YES, DOCTOR, I'M IN GREAT PAIN."

"WHAT PAINS YOU?"

"DOCTOR, I'M PAINED IN SPIRIT. I'M CONFUSED BY THE WORLD AROUND ME. LIFE DEPRESSES ME. NOTHING REALLY MAKES ME HAPPY. IN SHORT, I HAVE NOTHING TO LIVE FOR."

"I HAVE JUST THE CURE FOR YOU," REPLIED DR. HAMILTON. "WHAT YOU NEED IS A FEW GOOD LAUGHS, TO GET SOME PLEASURE OUT OF LIFE."

"BUT HOW?"

"THE CIRCUS IS IN TOWN THIS WEEK. GO TO SEE GRIMALDI. HE'S THE FUNNIEST MAN ON EARTH. HE'LL CURE YOU."

"DOCTOR," SAID THE MELANCHOLY MAN, "I AM GRIMALDI."

* * *

Men and women by the millions hide their inner confusion day after day behind Grimaldi-like smiles. Trying desperately to convince others that they've "arrived," they cover up a secret chaos that refuses to depart. Like the nerve-sizzling groans inside an amusement park haunted house, this chaos roars inside of them as mental racket, which includes self-punishing voices, stormy memories, riotous reactions, pleading insecurities, and make-believe arguments with absent antagonists.

Albert Blackburn's WORLDS BEYOND THOUGHT is a direct, no-nonsense guide out of haunted-house thinking. It clearly points the way out of the manic riot of habit-heavy thinking and towards the magical quiet of self-commanding Awareness. Personal experimentation with Blackburn's approach has convinced me of its sublime practicality. There is nothing more practical than to learn how to stop being a problem to oneself!

I first spoke to Al by telephone after reading his book NOW-CONSCIOUSNESS. Like all authentic truth teachers, Al evinced the spontaneous humility of one who had seen through the ego's sideshow of illusions. When he told me that he and his wife Gabriele would be driving through the Bay Area soon, I expressed my eagerness to meet him. "You're going to be very disappointed," came the reply, "I'm really just a nobody."

I wasn't disappointed.

In fact, in that meeting and in subsequent discussions, I discovered vital clues to self-realization in his Now-Consciousness philosophy that had eluded me during a decade of serious religious inquiry, an inquiry that had brought me into contact with many of the most renowned truth teachers of our time.

"A good man," wrote the Roman Poet Martial, "is always a beginner." Martial's words briefly suggest the quality of newness Al brought to every discussion of life. Seven of these shackle-shattering dialogues appear in WORLDS BEYOND THOUGHT. In them you'll discover an understanding of spiritual truth which differs from memorized metaphysical concepts in the same way the Milky Way differs from an unstruck paper match. A story will clarify this idea further.

In an obscure corner of the globe there once existed a bizzare society whose members carried a piece of rather ludicrous luggage everywhere they went. Each satchel contained figurines of human beings, life-like dolls that were far, far deadlier than the voodoo dolls of the Haitian jungle. Unlike voodoo dolls, these dolls didn't get stuck by pins. Instead, *they stuck their owners with confused lives, phony problems, and nightmarish notions.* They were, in fact, *Psoodoo Dolls* ("pseudo" being the Latin root for 'false'), for day after day these life-stealing statuettes embroiled their unlucky owners in false living.

Every community member had a personalized collection of Psoodoo Dolls, each fashioned in the image of someone known to its collector. There were dolls of husbands, dolls of wives, children dolls, in-law dolls, boss dolls, and co-worker dolls. In addition, each person's suitcase contained hundreds of miniatures sculpted in accordance with their owner's self-image.

The citizens of this society played in private with their Psoodoo Dolls at every possible opportunity. They'd reenact depressing scenes of times past with these preposterous puppets, and dream up soap-opera like fiascos cast in the unknown future. Thus they spent their days in useless mental agitation, virtually sleepwalking and sleeptalking through life. In fact, they were so obsessed with their doll-play that they propped these Psoodoo Dolls on their dashboards and drove home after work with haunted gazes fixed on these tiny terrors.

Then one day a teacher of truth came among them, and addressed them as a crowd. "Look," he said, "how you've twisted life into a grotesque nightmare. Your days have become psychological torture chambers, different only in the multifarious ways you devise to hurt yourselves."

Most of the crowd didn't understand him, many booed and yelled insults, but one person called out above the noisy assembly, "I know what you're talking about! You've accurately described my life. What can I do to end this horror?"

"Go to the river on the outskirts of town," replied the teacher, "and throw in your Psoodoo Dolls. Let it carry them away, along with their insidious, absurd dramas. Then you will know new life. You will discover an astonishing freedom and the delight of true relationships. And very soon something unexpected will happen: you will come upon a myserious, quiet awareness of unfathomable richness. This is not for me to describe. You will come face to face with it."

The others left and some were heard to whisper, "He isn't completely wrong, but rather than throw the figurines away, let's just not think of them for one hour on Sunday." Still another proposed, "What we should do is to add more religious dolls to our collections!" So soon, in this manner, most forgot the truth teacher's words, and continued in their nightmare.

Two or three, however, took the wise man's advice seriously. They tossed their Psoodoo Dolls into the River of Life and went from noise to newness.

* * *

Albert Blackburn was like that teacher of higher truth, urging those who sought his counsel to discover for themselves the heaven-sent poise of Now-Consciousness. His pleasantly relaxed manner, quiet self-command, and disarming lack of pretense silently informed those lucky enough to have known him that Al was living the truth of Jesus's words, "The Kingdom of heaven is within you." I never left his company without feeling mended, healed.

"All serious daring," observed Eudora Welty, "starts from within." WORLDS BEYOND THOUGHT is a book of serious daring. It is a panegyric to life triumphant, a cup from an everlasting Well not made by the toil of man, a Well which forever invites the thirsty.

JOE CONTI
LOS GATOS, CALIFORNIA

PART I

SEVEN CONVERSATIONS

The seven conversations that comprise Part I of WORLDS BEYOND THOUGHT are revised and expanded versions of actual dialogues that took place between Albert Blackburn and his wife Gabriele in their home in Ojai, California, dialogues which Idylwild Books subsequently made available on cassette recordings under the title FURTHER EXPLORATIONS INTO NOW-CONSCIOUSNESS. Prior to his death in June of 1987, Mr. Blackburn spent months carefully reviewing transcripts of these conversations, editing and revising the text, expanding and clarifying key ideas, and making certain that whatever changes had to be made to bring the text into conformance with the conventions of a written format did not modify or distort his basic ideas. These helpful elucidations and emendations make WORLDS BEYOND THOUGHT a completely new work in many respects, and one moreover in which Albert Blackburn's revolutionary insights are particularly accessible to the reader.

Monday

NOW-CONSCIOUSNESS

*Living in the present moment is beyond thought,
outside of human consciousness; it is living
in order, living a truly religious
life, a holistic life.*

G: Al, as you know, people are now involved in many New-Age movements, self-improvement movements, growth movements, and so on. There's a whole variety store available for people; a new workshop and seminar is being offered every week, everything from A to Z — from Astrology to Zen. Each of them promises something for its participants, and many imply that if you go through that particular method or system you will find reality, you will become enlightened, you will raise the *kundalini,* you will become a Master, and so on. It all seems so easy; if you do this, then you will become that. A lot of people are listening to all of this. What relationship does any of this have to now-consciousness?

A: I feel that there is a great deal of confusion concerning all of these things. Obviously there must be confusion, because there are so many individuals and organizations sending out literature. We get new announcements of these everyday, saying that if you follow our particular method it is going to lead you to reality and to all of the other things that go with it. I think part of the confusion stems from the fact that people may not know what they want out of life, and I think that is a good starting point.

Shouldn't everyone who is searching ask themselves, "What do I really want out of life? Do I want the real thing, and am I capable of perceiving the real thing if it comes along? Am I satisfied to experience only the result of ideas that either I or other people have created?" In other words, do I want to experience only the results of a certain system or method, to achieve a premeditated goal, or am I willing to see the facts as they are, and to accept those facts as they are?

G: I don't think people know. I think that people just believe that they are going to achieve an ultimate happiness, an ultimate enlightenment, and they will try anything to be happy. They think that truth is some end result, and after doing many other things they will reach it.

A: Don't most of these systems fall into two distinct categories? The first category would include the occult tradition, while the second category would involve mysticism, which is the religious approach, the approach of the mystics and the saints. I think that most of the things that we see advertised, most of the methods and meditation practices, fit into one or the other of these two categories. Wouldn't it be a good idea to define exactly what these two systems actually mean, as far as dictionary meaning is concerned?

G: Yes.

A: Because your idea of what constitutes occultism or mysticism will probably differ from mine; each person will have a different opinion. So in order to arrive at a clear definition, one with which most people can agree, we have to go to the dictionary.

Upon looking up occultism, I find that the meaning given is as follows: "a belief in hidden or mysterious powers and the possibility of subjecting them to human control." Mysticism is defined as "a theory postulating the possibility of direct and intuitive acquisition of ineffable knowledge or power." I think that those two definitions, those two categories, will fit almost all of the psychic and so-called "spiritual development" movements that are constantly being presented.

I think that both occultism and mysticism have several things in common. One common denominator is that they are both dualistic in nature, because in order to have a belief there has to be a believer, someone who is believing in a particular system. This entails time; it brings in the past and the future, and ignores the present. The past and future are concerned with time, and are products of thought, based upon memory and imagination.

G: Both approaches also emphasize the gaining of knowledge in order to have power.

A: The gaining of knowledge is related to time. In other words, I don't have knowledge today, but through a certain procedure or system of thought I will gain knowledge in the future, and that will hopefully bring the happiness or pleasure that I'm seeking. So it involves the dualistic approach, it involves time, it involves the past and the future, but not the present.

These two are the recognized methods which practically everyone follows, and all of the New-Thought movements (from my point of view), all of the systems of meditation, all of the different ideas and programs and seminars that are concerned with the so-called altering of the states of consciousness, giving you a higher state of consciousness, all are concerned with one or the other of these two methods.

Now-consciousness, as I speak of it, equates with awareness. If I look up awareness in the dictionary, I find that it is not concerned with time, because awareness is in the present. The definitions of awareness as given in the dictionary are as follows: "to be cognizant, to be conscious, to be sensible, to be alive, to be awake, and to be aware." All of these are in the present. They are non-dualistic because they are not talking about a "becoming" of any kind. They all concern a state of being, in each moment of time.

Maybe we can go on from there. I would like to have this very clear, because I think many people spend a tremendous amount of time thinking that they are going to get a particular result from what they are doing, and after spending years at it, they find out that it is a dead-end street. In my own case, for instance, I spent ten years in the intensive study of occultism in conjunction with a particular organization that I once belonged to — and to me it was a dead-end street. I didn't achieve the results that I hoped I would achieve. I think that many people find themselves in this position.

If people could know ahead of time what they were really looking for, they could settle for it. If they were interested in occultism, interested in arousing the *kundalini*, developing psychic powers, 'bouncing around between the planets,' having cosmic consciousness, et cetera, then occultism would be the route to follow. They could then do all kinds of miraculous feats to show off to others, be able to do all of the things that are supposed to be possible to accomplish by following that procedure. They could settle for that and not waste any time on now-consciousness or awareness. They could study astrology, and from that they could predict whether it was a good day to buy a new automobile, whether it was a propitious day to begin a certain activity, or whether so and so was going to be enamored with you that day and turned off on some other day — all of these things. Those are some of the things that supposedly can be gained through occult methods.

I consider most religious practices, most religious ceremonies, to be occult in nature, because the purpose of the ceremony is to bring about certain results at the psychic level which will supposedly bring down some power — the power of God, the power of Jesus, or some other power of a Master — into the room so that you will feel it, you will be helped, and you will be guided by it. I think that this is primarily what religion is all about as it is practiced today. I'm not talking about true religion, because from my point of view there is a true religious feeling and a true religious life that can be led; however, that life is not concerned with what goes on in most of the churches, or in the so-called religious establishments.

In the mystic tradition, for instance, many people have adored saints. They have thought that living a saintly life will lead to peace, tranquillity, and union with God. They have believed that through a system of self-denial — denying the actual fundamental physical and psychological drives within their nature — their goal will be reached. These ideas have led many to seclude themselves in a monastery or religious retreat. That lifestyle obviously requires an extreme dedication and a strong willpower to resist worldly temptations. Those who have succeeded in their quest have perpetuated the saintly tradition. However, if we read about the lives of saints objectively, we find that some of them have lived rather peculiar lives. Many literally starved themselves physically in order to induce visions, and certain systems of meditation were used to induce so-called religious experiences.

G: They tortured themselves in all kinds of ways.

A: Especially in India; this is still being done, all to find what is thought to be God and peace. I'm questioning whether you can find God or peace by torturing yourself, or by living an unnatural life. I believe that a person can get results from either of these two methods, if they want to; they can become occultists, and be looked up to by their fellows as magicians, psychics, clairvoyants, and so on, or they can become mystics, and by self-denial live a lifestyle that might be foreign to their nature and devoid of creative expression.

But isn't there another way of living that has more sanity, more logic, more factual benefit than either of these two approaches? That's what I am addressing myself to at the present. I think that it is very important because of what I found out in my own life. As I said before, I spent ten years involved in occultism, and there was also a time when I considered myself a mystic by nature, and I remember even making that statement on one or two occasions. Now I see that I wasn't an occultist, and I wasn't a mystic. Now I'm interested in the plain facts of life. What are they? Can we explore this together?

G: Yes. Now, do you think that any of what people are doing today is valuable in the sense of groundwork? People are talking a great deal about improving themselves, knowing themselves, knowing who they are; knowing what they want is what this usually means. Certainly the whole system of psychology has expanded into this area between religion and psychology. In fact, the two areas have merged. People think that by going through the pain and peculiarities of their neurotic behavior — all that psychology has talked about since Freud and Jung — that they will discover an easier way of life, and be able to let go of some of the pain or some of their problems by analyzing what they have done all of their lives.

Next they go into more occult areas, and try to find out about their past lives. So everything is getting mixed up; as you say, everything is merging. But I'm wondering about this: most people believe that if they do some of the groundwork, they are going to improve themselves, change themselves, expand themselves. Is that true, or are they just moving a little bit within their own field of consciousness?

A: Yes, they are. In addition, we have now achieved the capability to destroy ourselves. One person pushing the wrong button could destroy the world; it could be the beginning of the nuclear holocaust. So, if that's what we want — if we're satisfied with technology, and if we're satisfied with what scientists have found out about manipulating the physical aspects of our planet, to make more and more things out of certain elements — then fine.

But I don't feel that the people who are interested in the things that you and I are talking about (i.e., the people who are subscribing to these various methods of meditation or self-improvement, going to seminars, or spending money on this sort of thing) are primarily interested in that. At least it is only a secondary issue.

G: No, of course not; they are talking about fitness or their own health. They are also talking about world peace, saving the whales, wildlife, nature, and so on. That's all part of the new-age consciousness as well. Very few people are really happy with the world the way it is, and so there's this tremendous seeking going on.

A: People have a real hunger for some meaning in their lives. Don't you feel that we still come back to the question of what it is we want out of life? Obviously, if we want health and fitness, then many of the exercises that are taught, many of the systems of bodily training that are available, are obviously an aid to achieving that end. Similarly, if we are interested in changing the frequency rate of our psychic response to reality, then we can follow the methods set forth by the traditional occultists, and we can probably achieve that result, or some approximation of it. We can find out enough about it to see that those techniques might have that kind of result. If we want to be mystics, we can go to a monastery and abstain from sex, abstain from enjoyable foods, abstain from enjoyable conversation, deny our natural physical inclinations, and achieve a certain result. But we are talking now about something else, we're talking about something on a deeper level.

G: Can that level be reached through meditation? Meditation is now being promoted as having tremendous promise, and many people are meditating. They don't quite know what they are doing, but they take time, they sit down, and they are told (over and over again by many groups of people) that meditation will produce an altered state of consciousness. So that's again part of your 'becoming.' It is something that people are doing as easily as they are going out jogging and exercising. It is just so prevalent, and people really believe that they are going to gain peace of mind, have a happier or quieter day, be more capable of getting through their day, or be more capable of handling their problems. That is all part of what is going on at present.

A: I think that ground covered by the word meditation has expanded to exaggerated proportions, far beyond that encompassed by the term's original meaning and intent. From my point of view, anyone who creates anything in this physical world that we live in has to meditate about it first. For example, take the chair that I am sitting in, the chair that you are sitting in; somebody 'meditated' thought about that chair, figured out the porportions of it, the size of it, the height of it and the width of it, before the chair actually came into physical existence. Someone had to do this. Somebody dreamed up the outline of that chair in their minds; they meditated about it, and the meditation was brought to fruition by the people who constructed and actually manufactured the chair. Everything that you see in this room which is man-made was meditated upon and is a result of meditation. Obviously, meditation of that kind works; and if it works with physical things, then it certainly must work in other areas as well.

I can sit down and, through concentration, force my mind to reject all of the extraneous ideas that come to it. Hopefully, I'll reach a state where I absolutely have it under control, and think of just one thing so strongly that I actually visualize what I'm thinking about. I may see it as a visualization, as a vision — and then I say it is real because I've seen it.

You may sit down and visualize the face of a Master, or the face of a teacher, or whatever you wish, and if you do this long enough in a very concentrated way, you can project your image to the point where you really see it. But what have you actually done? You have taken the immaterial substance of the psychic level, the thought level, and you have brought all of that together into an image which you either see inwardly as an idea, or see projected as a vision. My point is this: Does this have any relationship to enlightenment and spiritual regeneration?

Personally, I would like to go much deeper into this. I'm no longer satisfied with dreaming up something and then experiencing my own creation, because it has no substance to it, so far as changing my true relationship with my family, with my friends, or with the environment in which I have to live.

G: So the euphoric experiences, the expanded-consciousness experiences, the drug-induced experiences — are you saying that all of that is illusion?

A: No, I'm not saying it is illusion, I'm saying that it is using the material within human consciousness.

I think at this particular point we ought to say what human consciousness is. To me, it consists of all of the material that has been created and added to by human beings through countless ages. It is the sum total of what we have thought, felt, and experienced; all of the edited material, the rerun material, the censored material; all of the experiences that we humans have gone through over the ages. This is the sum total of human consciousness.

My feeling is that any meditation that is done, or any thought that is used by us on the conscious level (the conscious level as we know it), is utilizing this material. It is the rearranging of this material so that you can transmute it into the physical world — either in the form of a chair, a boat, an airplane, an automobile, a vision of the Master, or an idea — that is accomplished through the popular forms of so-called meditation.

G: It could also be a spirit guide, a teacher, someone from the other side of death. So you are saying that if you sit down purposefully to meditate, you are going to tune into the vast storehouse of human consciousness, thought-forms, and all that man has known or dreamed of.

A: In other words, you are rearranging the known. The known is the content of human consciousness . . .

G: And you are not touching that which is beyond.

A: No, from my point of view virtue, enlightenment, true understanding, love, and any other of those qualities that we are seeking through these various methods, are not to be found within this area of human consciousness as we know it, except as ideas.

We have spent a lot of time so far discussing the methods traditionally recommended as ways to approach truth, and I think that we should perhaps approach the subject on a deeper level. Obviously, we can't discuss the unknown, but we can discuss some of the obstacles facing us and consider what prerequisites, if any, are necessary before one can actually experience something beyond the content of human consciousness. Because this is what all of these systems promise. They promise enlightenment, or an experience of unitive consciousness; in fact, they promise all kinds of things. I question whether these systems could actually achieve their goal. If the goal is known, which it would have to be in order for any system or method to be promulgated to attain it, it must be included within human consciousness already. You can't promote a system about something that is unknown; it is impossible.

G: Even if you call it mystical?

A: No matter what you call it — a mystic approach, an occult approach, a meditative approach, or a scientific approach — all are within the field of the known. In following a particular system you might achieve its premeditated goals, but you can not touch the unknown.

Now, what is outside of human consciousness? Everything that you can think about, everything that you can talk about, everything that you can discuss is within the field of consciousness. All of philosophy, all of religion, all of the content of books, all of the knowledge in the libraries and the universities, everything is within the field of the known. Now, is it possible to go beyond that? This is the question that I am interested in, because I see that in following all of the methods and systems of religion and philosophy, we have not bettered our condition. Wars have gotten bigger, and conflicts between nations have gotten more intense. The proliferation of nations has gone on and on, with big nations splitting up into two or three smaller nations, each one separate, each one thinking that it is unique, that it has the truth, and each warring constantly with others. So I see that none of the information that is available to me within human consciousness is going to take me out of the known into the state of peace, tranquillity, love, and understanding that is promised. It is a false hope.

G: Let's be absolutely clear. You think that there is no value at all in studying, or pursueing, or learning about these methods?

A: There's a value if you are satisfied with superficial results. If you are satisfied with rearranging the pieces within human consciousness so that you can temporarily live in harmony with a certain situation, then I say that they do have value because they can give you temporary relief. A war, for instance, temporarily relieves the tension between two nations because one is on top of the other and the other can't move. The tension between two individuals, for instance a man and a wife, may be relieved if they go to a marriage counselor or a psychologist — perhaps their tension is eliminated entirely. Sometimes it is eliminated by the psychologist advising the couple to split up and find other partners; or they are given new terms to apply to their situation, and if they are satisfied with the new terms, there is a relief of tension. Obviously there are superficial results to be gained from everything that humanity has done. If I want a stronger body, then I can exercise and get a stronger body; I can do all of these things. But we're going beyond this now; we are trying to achieve something different, to find a true solution to our psychological problems.

Those few who are interested in true inner peace — a life without conflict, a state of well-being, a state of love, a feeling of unity, sacredness, and understanding moment by moment, that does not change and is not altered by circumstances — such people have to approach the problem in a different way.

G: And there is no path to that!

A: How can there be a path to it? The things that were mentioned in regard to awareness can only take place in the present. You can not be cognizant in the future, you can not be conscious, sensible, alive, awake, or aware in the future or the past. It is all in the present moment. You can not love somebody in the future or in the past. You can not understand something in the future or in the past. You can not have a feeling for the sacredness of life in the future or the past. You can not have a feeling of unity between you and everything surrounding you in the past or in the future. All of these things take place moment by moment by moment, and from my point of view are part of this energy that we call life, the thing we call universal mind. You can name it God, you can call it whatever you want to call it, but all of those qualities are only found in the present moment.

So the present moment is outside of human consciousness, and it's the only thing that is. It is only brought into the realm of human consciousness when we name or evaluate any part of it. It is so simple, but instead of letting it remain simple we are always doing something with it. Out of the millions of bits of information available to us at each moment, we pick and choose only particular fragments of the totality of that present moment. We do this because it is part of our conditioning, it is our way of behaving. The brain cells that have been activated through usage, as a consequence of the lifestyle which we live, allow us to recognize only fragments of the totality and potentiality of the present. So instead of living in the present moment and assimilating, perceiving, under-standing, and being aware of this totality, to the extent that we are personally capable of being, we identify with a certain little bit of the information that is there, a certain fragment of it, and from then on we are completely oblivious to any pos-sible intuitive feeling for the totality and what it holds for us.

The present moment is holistic; it is the state that every-body is seeking because it is a totality, it is a whole. Living in the present moment means really living a holistic life in its true sense, because it pertains to every facet of life, not just one little part. It is not running off into occultism, or mysti-cism, or astrology, or science, or chemistry, or something else. It is learning to live factually, and being able to respond factu-ally through whatever action is necessary.

If one can live this way, one becomes an artist in living, an artist in life rather than an artist in painting a picture, being a musician, or even being a nuclear scientist. In other words, do not be bound by a certain paradigm that pertains to only one small interest in life, but have a total interest in everything that comes along, and respond totally as far as you can to whatever comes along.

G: You are saying that one should lay aside the belief, the hope, the carrot that is dangled in front of you, because all these other ways, all these paths, will not lead to truth; lay these aside and really investigate your life, your 'what is,' your present state of being?

A: Right. Hope and belief don't enter the picture in the present moment. They only exist when you have identified with something and start explaining it, or understanding it, in terms of human consciousness, what people know. But your present moment is the unknown. You and I do not know exactly what is going to happen in the next moment. The present moment becomes the known through a thought process which is triggered by memory, which immediately names or evaluates it.

G: Most people would say, "I know my present moment: it is pain, it is confusion, it is a problem, it is all that I don't like about myself and all that I do like about myself, all that I want to change; therefore, I'm going to look for somebody to help me to change."

A: I think that most people would respond in that way. But in what you have just said, you're not describing the present moment, and if they responded in this way, they would not be responding to the present moment either, because all of those names that you gave are conditioned responses that have been programmed into the content of consciousness. These form a part of our personal consciousness, part of human consciousness. At this present moment, you could not be feeling all of those things that you just mentioned. You could not be feeling frustration, you could not be feeling anger, because any of those things that you might be feeling would have to be named in order for you to tell me about them. In other words, at the moment that you were telling me that you were angry, you couldn't tell me that you were confused; and when you were telling me that you were confused, you couldn't tell me that you were frustrated.

G: I understand, but most people would say, "My life is like that; my life is confused, and I'm frustrated, and what shall I do about it?" It may sound like you are splitting hairs here.

A: But these things have nothing to do with the present moment. I will admit that someone's life might have been frustrating, might have been confusing, might have been painful, might have been all of these things in a linear way; sometimes a person's life might have been that way. But I am denying that it is possible to feel all of those things at this present moment in time. You can't do it, you can't feel it, because if you drop the name then the feeling is no longer there. The feeling that you are naming is only there at the time you're naming it. You say "I'm angry," and the minute you say "I'm angry," the word anger goes into your computer and out comes all of the things that used to make you angry, and this brings on a feeling of anger, which you then describe to me, but it is only there because you have named it. If you do not name any of these things, then you don't recall any of this material out of your memory bank, out of your consciousness; you only recall it when you name it. The name is the recall button that you push to bring this material out of your consciousness, in order to describe to me the feeling that you call anger. The mind works only in a linear way. You can only go from one name to another name, so you are bringing in time. Living only in the present moment is a timeless state; from a psychological point of view, it is a timeless state.

G: Someone listening is going to say, "Well, what am I going to do about my anger, my confusion, my pain, my desire for happiness, or enlightenment?"

A: If the significance of what I have just said has sunk in, and you are willing to experiment with it yourself, I think you will find that these things only exist when you have recalled them from your consciousness by naming them. If you do not name them they're not there. The name corresponds to the recall button on a recorder. What you can do is to wake up to the fact that you have just pushed the recall button on anger; you've just named anger. As soon as you see the significance of this process and how it really works psychologically, you'll realize that the minute you name something you have established a link with that particular part of your consciousness. If you have really seen that this is true, then every time you catch yourself pushing the button, every time you catch yourself saying "I'm angry," you drop it; every time you catch yourself saying "I'm frustrated," you drop it. You have to realize that you are the one who is pressing this button by naming it. If you don't name the feeling, if you stay right in the present moment, it doesn't have a name. The present moment is unknown, it is brand new, fresh, clean, and so on. If you can stay with that, then you're out of it, you're automatically free.

   Thus there is no such thing as *karma; karma* is your conditioning. People use the word *karma* to explain, or to justify, all kinds of actions. They justify killing and being-killed by using this word *karma,* and it is an exotic word. It is actually conditioning, this computerized naming that we insert into our consciousness. But naming drops away effortlessly the moment you are aware of your action, although I think you first have to see what happens when you name something, and realize that you're creating the link and are automatically stuck with the results.

G: That's clear, but just dropping the name doesn't get rid of the violence, or the anger, or the jealousy.

A: It does, for in that moment you're not violent or jealous or angry; you're only experiencing the result of whatever the last button was that you pushed. Most people try to escape their jealousy by pushing another button. In other words, we are constantly changing the state of our feelings and of our experiencing of life by means of the different names that we use; there are all of these buttons that we have learned, the names of all these things. But if you do not name something, what is it in the present moment? You might have a certain feeling, but when you discover the source of that feeling, it might turn out to be something completely different than you thought, and a true transmutation can take place.

G: Yes, I see what you are talking about now. You're not implying that simply not naming something will immediately turn you into a saint because you have dropped it. Some psychological problems do not go away that easily.

A: I think we have sufficiently discussed that topic; I'd like to consider the following question now. What is a truly religious life? How can I discover for myself whether or not there is actually such a thing as a religious life? To answer this question I have to discard all of my ideas on the subject. If I apply any name whatsoever — for example, if I say that a religious life is peace, that a religious life is seeing visions, that a religious life is talking with God — if I name what a religious life is in any way, I am immediately linked to everything within human consciousness that is related to that particular idea. And what I obtain, what I discover, is the result of everything that my fellow man has thought on that subject for thousands of years — and it is not reality. But if I am really serious, I have to start very, very simply; I can't start at the top of the ladder.

I would like to relate this to something that anyone can experience for themselves. I think that in very simple things one can find a common denominator applicable to everybody. Truth and reality, the real and true things in life, are available to everyone. The air we breathe is available to everyone; the sunlight is available to everyone. All the things in this world that are a part of the natural order are available to everyone. So what I want to know is this: What is absolutely true for everyone, what can everyone actually relate to, even those people who have not read the occult books, have not read Krishnamurti, have not read anything of that nature? We can all experience the present moment, because that is available to everyone. The possibility of stepping out of human consciousness and participating in the factual reality of life, moment by moment, is theoretically open to everybody. But most people will not realize this because they are not interested in stepping out; they are interested in rearranging the pieces already within their consciousness. And in that particular direction, of course, is where so-called progress lies; it involves rearranging the pieces, assigning new names to them, splitting up the big pieces into little pieces, naming each individual piece, and so on. That's what we call progress. Let us go to something else.

Everything in this room was created by man — all of the objects, the furniture, everything here. But the minute you step outside into the natural order you are surrounded by things that were not created by man. You could say that those things are the creations of God, or the creations of the life-force, or the results of the evolutionary thrust of life.

G: Then when someone realizes this and lays aside all of these various ideas and methods, there is tremendous energy available for a new approach.

A: That's right. Obviously, a person's energy depends upon that person's physical health. But in addition, I think that most people's energy is spread very, very thin over many things; how thin depends upon their range of interests. Most people are interested in mentally escaping their self-created problems. We create our own problems, then spend our time trying to solve them! I think what is necessary is to look in all directions, be willing to look in whatever direction your interest leads you.

I spent years, for instance, in exploring different paths when I was interested in the occult tradition. I now see other people spending their lives searching, thinking they are going to find answers. I think perhaps what is necessary is to be able to see that there is no real answer, there is no lasting answer, no everlasting inner peace, or security, or love to be found in anything that is part of human consciousness.

G: And one begins by questioning in this way.

A: You have to question all of your accepted values. You have to be willing to question absolutely everything. You have to question all of your beliefs, and you have to question all other people's beliefs. This includes all knowledge. Technically speaking, we don't have to find out whether the formula that made a certain kind of steel is the correct formula; I'm not talking about that. But you have to be willing to investigate whether or not any of these methods of escaping our dilemma are of lasting benefit. Once you've done that, then I think you can look at what the present moment has to offer, without pushing all of those replay buttons in your personal computer, your brain.

G: Then what happens? How does that change your life? It is an entirely new approach, is it not?

A: Yes, and I feel it can be a very simple approach. Let us step out of human consciousness, figuratively speaking, and just open our eyes and see what happens. Let's step out of this door, get out into the sunshine; there we find ourselves surrounded by things that are not man-made, such as the trees, and the birds, and the flowers, and the animals, and all of the natural things. We find that there is a complete order ruling all of these particular creations, and to very simply become part of that order ourselves, we have to see how those creations live. We see that everything that exists there has a purpose. Everything that is not created by man, but by nature, has a purpose. And when it ceases to fulfill the purpose for which it was created, it goes out of existence; it does, it is destroyed, it is killed, it is eaten by some other animal, and so on. So the first step is to really observe. I have to bring that simplicity into my life.

How can I bring order into my life? First, I have to find out if there is any true value to the kind of a life that I'm living; does it have any purpose at all? Am I fulfilling in my everyday life and in my relationships what obviously is my particular responsibility? I can't expect to see the ultimate, to have cosmic consciousness, to have enlightenment, or achieve any of the other so-called ultimates that people have talked about, and still live the kind of life that most people live.

There must be a symbiotic relationship with the rest of the natural order.

An awareness of disorder is the beginning of true order in my life, and a radical change takes place. I have to create order in my life because I see that order is one of the fundamental laws that governs the entire universe. There must be order in my relationship to human consciousness, because while my mind is identified with disorder there is no quiet time in which to holistically understand life. Therefore, my life has to be orderly. I see that the universe is governed by all the things that are real and true; all of the so-called virtues are expressed in the natural order of the universe.

G: It is all that is good, all that is beautiful, all that is love.

A: I see that, so if there is to be an experiencing of truth, an experiencing of reality, I must bring this true understanding into my life. I have to go to the natural order and find out where my life is not in accordance with that order. I have to drop the things that I see do not fit into it; I have to tune my life to its frequency. It is not going to change its frequency and come down to my level and suddenly enlighten me, especially if I am living a completely disorderly, nasty, mean life. My life must be changed. There has to be a change in my frequency, so that my frequency will correspond with that of the natural order of things. And this change, I feel, is brought about through what I call pure perception, through being aware of the ways in which I am failing to live in harmony with the natural order of life.

I feel that anyone can do this. They don't need a seminar, they don't need a workshop; they need nothing except the ability to watch themselves moment by moment by moment, using now-consciousness.

DIRECT PERCEPTION

*To see without thought, memory, or any
past conditioning brings freedom and
touches that which is sacred
and eternal.*

G: It has been said many times throughout the ages that we must know ourselves. What does this mean to you?

A: In the first place, what do I mean by myself? I think that should be the first question, the initial inquiry into that particular subject. What do I mean by 'me?'

G: Everything that I think I am — my memories, my ideas about myself, my self-image, everything that I have collected during my life.

A: I think that most people have only a very hazy idea of what they are. I think it is a question that is very rarely asked: What am I? If you really ask that question seriously, and start investigating it, what can you pin down as yourself? Most people say "I'm my body;" all right, you could cut a finger off, and obviously the finger would not be you. You could cut your foot off, or your leg off, or anything else off, and that would obviously not be you. You could take any part of the body and put a piece of it under a microscope or magnifying glass and you might be able to see the cells of the body and all of that, but that isn't the real 'you.'

G: No.

A: So we can leave the body out, that's not 'me.' Then people might say, "Well, I am my thoughts." You can take any one of your thoughts and analyze each idea, each little word, each sentence, each feeling and meaning; that's obviously not you, because your thoughts are constantly changing as a result of any education that you obtain and the experiences of meeting and talking to other people. So if I'm not my body, and I'm not my thoughts, am I my feelings? Surely not, since my feelings also are constantly changing.

G: I think 'we' are the totality of our ideas and our self-images; and not just about ourselves, but about ourselves in relationship to what we have done and where we live, and our environment, our tribe, and our community. I am an accumulation of the many names that I've given myself.

A: Then would you say that the core of 'me' is memory?

G: Yes.

A: But the memories are very faulty, aren't they? Because we obviously don't remember the totality of the experiences that we've had, we just remember the highlights.

G: Yes.

A: And we conveniently forget the unhappy experiences that we've had; in some cases, these result in neurotic tendencies further along the line.

G: But we think that we are more than simply memory and the ability to rearrange memory with thought; we think there is something else.

A: Yes, we've agreed that the physical body is not the self, nor are thoughts the self, because they are constantly changing. In addition, memories are not the self because they obviously are composed of material that has been added to and deleted from since any experience actually happened.

G: As long as I hold on to all of that, it is part of what I call 'me.'

A: Yes, but what is the 'I' that is holding on to this? If it is not the body; if it is not the mind, not the mental part or the mental process; and if it is not the memories; then what is this thing that is putting all of this together and calling itself "I"?

G: The thinker, the observer, the one that's watching. And what is it that I'm watching?

A: No, the question should be, what is the watcher? Is there such a thing as the watcher? Is the watcher a fact, or is it also simply an idea?

G: Well, of course, as Krishnamurti says, the observer is the observed.

A: But that really is just an idea to most people; simply saying that the observer is the observed is an idea. It is not a fact until one has actually experienced it.

G: I'm also interested in this question: What is it that I think I'm observing all of the time? Am I wasting my time observing 'what is' and thinking about that, and adding it to my field of consciousness?

A: Vast numbers of people have been listening to Krishnamurti for many years, and I have heard some of them make the statement that Krishnamurti advocates watching your thoughts, because in watching your thoughts you will come to know yourself. And in knowing yourself, you will come to know the rest of the world and other people. I wonder if this is true, if Krishnamurti really said this, or whether he said something else. Personally, I find that it is impossible to watch my thoughts; there can only be awareness of the movement of thought.

G: What do you watch, then?

A: If you actually experiment with it yourself, I think that you will see that thought and observation can not go side by side, can not occur simultaneously.

G: Yes.

A: Therefore, if they can not occur simultaneously, obviously it must be impossible to watch your thoughts, and so you can not come to know yourself by this process, because it is based on an illusion to start with.

G: I can watch what I have just thought. I can say, "I just thought such and such, and wasn't that great, wasn't that silly," and so on.

A: That seems to be correct, because I find that I can suddenly become self-conscious of the fact that my thought has just been identifying with a certain idea, a certain prejudice, or a certain reaction to a challenge. I can suddenly wake up to this fact, and become self-aware or self-conscious that this has happened. In doing so, I erroneously believe that I'm watching thought. I'm not actually watching thought, I am watching the replay of the thought that I have just been engaged in rather than the thought itself. The happenings of life come to us unsolicited; we can't predict them, we can't change them, and we can't alter them even though we try. All of our self-protective thinking is based on the erroneous idea that we can bypass happenings in life, become immune to them, or side-step them in some way. But the harsh realities of life that happen to us unexpectedly — such as sudden death, accidents, the actions of other people, or natural catastrophes — we can not avoid. We have no way of shielding ourselves from all of these things, and when they happen we are devastated.

I wonder if we are completely awake when these things happen? My own feeling is that the present moment, the actual totality of each moment, is not perceived holistically by any of us, because there are too many things involved. As we said once before, there may be a thousand pieces of information available to us within each moment of time, within each happening, but we are limited by our thought processes and by our recognition processes. We are limited by our ideas, which all exist within the field of human consciousness. We are unable to perceive or to understand the totality of each given moment.

Our brain/consciousness is constantly seeking security. We feel insecure when unexpected happenings in life take place, when accidents or unforeseen events occur. So, when we feel insecure, there seems to be a shut-off mechanism which prevents us from seeing the totality of the moment. Instead, we change automatically into a different mode of thinking, involving what might be called a replay. While the happening is actually taking place there is a change in consciousness; instead of being aware of what is really happening, we substitute ideas based on memory, and we watch that instead of the actual event itself.

G: Do you think it is a self-protective switch? We are unable to cope with the challenge when it comes, so it is more convenient to file it and then go back to it at a later time when we think we might be less emotional about it?

A: That's exactly right; that's how it seems to be. Because the brain has to have security. We seek psychological security within the field of consciousness, the content of which is (as we said before) the totality of what everyone has thought and experienced over the millions of years that human beings have lived on this earth. All of this information is available to us; we can run it through our computer, which is the brain, and obtain an answer to a problem facing us. In other words, humanity has experienced all of these things, and somewhere along the line, someone has experienced a situation similar to the one we are now facing. It is similar in nature, but it is not identical, because new things have been added to it; as we said before, each moment is completely new.

G: You are now saying that it is the nature of the brain to not meet a challenge completely. Is that the only reason? Perhaps there are others. For example, we might find it more convenient to file something away and say I'll think about it later, or I'll work it out later, or I'll use my other capacities after I have evaluated the situation and decided whether I do or do not like it. There may also be other reasons why we rarely meet something in a completely fresh manner. Is it the nature of thought to play with things like that?

A: I don't believe that we go into any of this intellectualization at the time something happens; instead I think that we react automatically. We do not meet the challenge completely, with all of our sensitivity, or with all of our capabilities.

G: I understand that, but I'm trying to find out why. One of the reasons is conditioning. We've been conditioned to take time with everything; to rethink something, study it, ask other people, look in books, and then come to a conclusion. Our whole education stressed that approach. We are given a project, and then told to work on it for a while. As children we are informed that we lack knowledge, and told that when we grow up, when we are older, at some later time we will be able to understand things. Thus there is constant conditioning and education for postponement.

A: What we are using (that is, what we have to work with consciously) are the brain and the content of human consciousness. These have obviously developed through time, through the evolutionary process, over millions and millions of years. They are the products of time. The brain is the result of a linear step-by-step progression through the evolutionary process, while the content of consciousness is the material which has been filtered through the brain during the evolutionary process. Both have developed through time. Therefore,

31

the only instruments we have to operate with are both bound by time. But the present moment never exists in time; there is no psychological time connected with the present moment. So it exists in a different dimension, or there are other dimensions involved in the present moment that are not involved in the time process. Therefore, when we use limited instruments (such as the human brain and human consciousness) to understand an event that is happening in a moment out of time, we can not perceive the holistic nature of that moment. We can only see a fragment of it. The brain is aware of this, and so as a self-protective mechanism and to keep from feeling insecure, it has developed an automatic cutoff device. The moment that something happens with which the brain can not cope, it shuts off its receptiveness. It immediately draws information from its memory about similar situations. It plays this together with the actual happening, and our consciousness is immediately distracted from the actual happening. Attention is given to the replay, which is a part of our memory, because the brain can cope with that. It has dealt with it in the past, and has already explored all of the ramifications that go with it. Therefore, we rarely see a happening when it is taking place; we see a rerun of the happening that we have dredged up from our memory bank. If there are any new details that look a little different to us, we add those details and edit the film again, and put this new version in our memory bank for future reference. This stored material gives us the security of the 'known.'

G: So we're living with secondhand tapes!

A: Yes. We make a print of the film that we are using when we have it all edited or have it exactly the way we want it, arranged very neatly in accordance with our prejudices and ideas. That print is then put in our memory bank, and it is what is pulled out the next time a similar situation arises. Thus each time we look at an edited film, and that's how we meet most life situations. In other words, the events in our lives are perceived and reacted to through this screen of conditioning.

Events are always perceived in a two dimensional way, because a film is two dimensional; it has height and width but no depth. In other words, the life quality which is intrinsic in each happening (such as understanding, love, or any of the other qualities of life) is not inherent in the film. It is only inherent in the actual happening itself. The actual happening is multidimensional, while the rerun or replay material is only two-dimensional.

G: Right. But what you're saying is that we also keep altering the replayed material. We take a replayed film and act another little scene in front of it, and then that is photographed again, so that the two are merged together. Thus we're constantly refilming, or reediting, or retaping, adding track upon track to create what thought seems to think is security. We compare our imagery with other people's behavior and modify it a little here, or change it a little there. If it seems to be all right and is accepted by our society, by our peers, or by the tribe or community we are living in, we feel more secure; we cling to this reedited material, because other people have done the same thing. They recognize the material, accept it, and play the same game.

A: Do you realize that if you see the dynamics of this conditioning process, it is the first step towards freedom from the 'known?'

G: So everything reinforces this process! Am I filled with tapes and images?

A: That is what comprises human consciousness; it is composed of all of the edited material, all of the reruns of our life experiences. This material comprises the contents of our memory banks. And when we apply this material to life situations, we consider ourselves to be living intelligently. The more of this kind of information we have, the more sophisticated or educated we feel ourselves to be, but (from my point of view) the less qualified we are to live creatively. A child is more vulnerable to life; a child's memory bank is not filled with conditioned material. However, the mind of somebody who has lived fifty or sixty years may be frozen in concrete as a result of having absolute faith in this material and believing that this material will show them how to cope with any situation that might come up. But obviously they can not cope, because we see most people living chaotic lives.

G: Is there any point in observing all of this? Do you not get endlessly lost in watching replays of all of your tapes?

A: Let me introduce another point while we are still on this subject. If the perspective we are discussing has any validity, then it is rather scary to realize that we are all governed by history; and what we call history is the remembered, altered, edited experiences and limited points of view that we human beings have passed down from generation to generation. All of history — the history of certain people, the history of society, ways of acting, ways of dealing with situations — all of this consists of very limited, edited personal material.

G: Organized methods of doing things.

A: Yes. In addition, wars between people, misunderstandings between one society and another, one nationality and another, are also based upon this limited, edited material. We can't deal rationally with the Russians because our ideas get in the way; we don't see the Russians as they really are, and the Russians don't see Americans as they really are.

G: It is all because of the ideas, and images, and propaganda that have been put out, of course.

A: It is also because of the fact that everything has been edited for personal reasons, personal biases, or for personal gain in influencing economic situations. For instance, it is not economically to our advantage to get along with certain people. It is not economically advantageous to get along with the Nicaraguans, or the Russians, or whoever our so-called 'enemies' happen to be at a particular time.

G: At least, that is what the politicians would like us to believe!
    But let us get back to two people meeting and trying to communicate through the screen of conditioning. Each one is pulling out his rerun tapes; that is what happens in a relationship.

A: That's right, each person creates an image of the other person. For example, husbands and wives have images of each other. In the very beginning, they see the other person as their ideal; after they marry, their images gradually change.

G: So they either modify their tapes some more, or they decide that it is not possible to change further and they can't live together anymore.

A: It seems that way to me, because in observing myself and my own life, I see that unless I'm completely awake, completely attentive, and completely aware, it is not possible to conceptually grasp the depth or the multidimensional nature of each moment. So the question is, how can I perceive it completely; this can only be done when the brain, the computerized recording machine, is bypassed, and therefore the programmed material in it is also bypassed. Only then is there a direct perception of the uniqueness, the beauty, and the completeness of the given moment, including the events and challenges and any occurrences in my life.

To me, life can be approached in either of these two ways. There can be a perception that is completely of the moment and which is multidimensional, in which there is love, understanding, feeling, compassion, and generosity, in which there is an understanding and forgiveness of the other person, and a forgiveness of yourself if you're involved in some way. All of those responses are complete. Events can be met in that way, or they can be met in the way that is usually done: incompletely, with thought, and through the brain mechanism which is two-dimensional and time related. You can dip into human consciousness, drag out what you think is the appropriate memory to correspond with the happening, and then deal with the situation using that programmed material as a guide.

G: The interesting thing about what you're saying is this: When you live in the moment and do not pull out your edited tapes, when you meet a challenge in the moment, you are not making a new tape; no memory is created.

A: That's right; the event leaves no mark. It does not add to the content of human consciousness because you've bypassed it.

36

G: That's why sometimes you can't remember what you have said or thought or done, because the moment was complete! You can't go back to it and say, this is how I felt, or that is what I said, because there was so much involved. You simply met the challenge and it vanished. So what happens to the brain? I know it doesn't like any of this very much. It would much prefer that you made a new tape.

A: It seems to be a fact that the brain needs security to develop; the activation of new brain cells requires security, doesn't it? Because if there is insecurity, there is a feeling of danger, there is a feeling of being threatened. Thus the brain will be busy trying to alleviate the feeling of insecurity, trying to establish a balance, an order, so that there will be harmony. This is a fact. But if the brain is physically and psychologically secure, then I feel that the thrust of the life-force, which is expressing itself through everything, will develop the brain cells and keep them functioning in a healthy, normal manner.

In addition, most of us live in very narrow patterns; our lives become very narrow because of our limited interests, and because of our prejudices. Living a narrow life and being oblivious to everything except the things that we are interested in requires the use of only a certain number of brain cells; few are required for responding in a programmed way to a narrow lifestyle.

G: We don't need very many to simply repeat all of the things we're familiar with.

A: No, the habitual actions or thoughts that most of us engage in require only a limited number of brain cells; the rest are inactive. It has been said that most people need only ten percent of their potential brain capacity to function in our society. Therefore, it would seem reasonable to me that if someone were to be aware of reality moment by moment, and was capable of perceiving at least a part of the millions of bits of information that are available in each moment, his or her life would be greatly enriched. The perception of more of the details of life would also engender an interest in more things. If you are no longer narrowly focussed on one particular concern and are awake to the totality that is the moment, there are many, many more things in which to be interested. You may become aware of and interested in the flowers, the trees, the birds, and how nature functions in particular ways. In other words, many new interests come into being in conjunction with the state of perception or awareness, and new brain cells must necessarily be activated in order to cope with the additional information.

G: It would seem that a state of perception creates the energy to activate new brain cells. In addition, a broadening of one's life and an increased interest in living, in relationships, in understanding — all of these would activate new brain cells. However, if one lived only with the replay mechanism, I think one would use fewer and fewer cells, and would end up senile, frozen, or crystalized when one was old.

A: That raises the question of the computer, and the possible effects it may have on the brain. The brain is a result of millions of years of conditioning. It is a result of the actions, experiences, and reactions to challenges of different organisms over millions of years. Life has offered challenges and the brain has responded to these challenges in a linear way. There has been an actual evolutionary growth of the brain's capacity to respond to these challenges through the ages; it has developed through actually having to face things. The brain has not developed through ideas. It has developed as a consequence of having to cope factually at any given moment with whatever physical challenge happened to exist.

G: You have to include abstract thinking as part of that development as well.

A: Yes, but now we have the computer, so instead of meeting a challenge personally, we let the computer meet the challenge. When I was a boy many years ago, and I was asked a mathematical question or any other question, I had to actually utilize my brain in order to figure out the answer. It was a direct challenge, and as a result of the effort required to come up with the answer, my brain cells were activated at that particular time. I don't know if there was actual physical growth or if existing cells were simply activated, but something occurred as a result of the question that I had been asked. I had to personally come up with an answer.

Now, in school, many kids have their personal little calculators and computers, and they are taught how to press the right button on the computer. It takes very little effort for the brain to learn, in a mechanical way, which button to press. It is like learning to type; you don't have to think about each letter, it is all automatic. The same thing applies to the computer.

What is happening to the brain during all of this? Isn't it conceivable that we will become more and more mechanical in our thinking? In other words, there won't be any creative thinking anymore, because something mechanical is not creative. So where will creativity enter into our learning to function in this computerized society and age that we're living in? Will the brain cells that were used to solve concrete challenges in the past degenerate, will they just become quiescent as they are no longer used? What will happen to society? I don't think it requires too great a stretch of the imagination to see what is happening. We see that people are less and less creative; they are more and more imitative. Instead of going out and spending time playing baseball themselves, they watch a baseball game on TV. Instead of playing football themselves, they watch the game on TV. Everything is becoming more and more imitative.

G: Secondhand sports.

A: Secondhand sports, secondhand exercise, secondhand everything. Of course this obviously doesn't involve everybody, because there are people who are producing the things that other people watch; there are football players out there playing football. But they are certainly in the minority compared to the people watching the game.

G: Yesterday, I saw a news report on TV about what toys are going to be like in the future. They are going to be more and more mechanical, with more video games both for children and adults. Experts foresee little robots for children to play with, so that they will have mechanical playmates. That will be very nice; they will get robots to clean up their rooms for them instead of doing it themselves. They will also get the robots to respond to them the way they want them to. This will take them further and further away from real interplay with other children. You can see what this is going to do to relationships, to the learning process involved in children growing up together. Instead of naturally taking a walk together, children will have their little robots that will be all programmed for them to play with.

A: Of course, the problem is this — what you or I think or feel about the situation is not going to change it, because mechanization is obviously going to continue as far as it can, because it will make work easier for people. People are going to have more leisure time for sports and games, and for playing around or doing what they want. But the things that they will be doing are not going to be the kinds of things that will bring about a further development of the brain. Instead, they will bring about a deterioration or a degeneration of many of the brain cells that have been necessary up to now.

G: So people themselves are becoming more and more like robots.

A: Right.

I think that we should get back to the original question about understanding ourselves. I wonder if we have discussed everything related to that subject?

G: What we have discussed is certainly part of understanding what is going on within ourselves.

A: Don't most of us have an idea that we are some wonderful thing that is sort of untouchable; that is everlasting, eternal, immortal. If a person is religious, he or she feels that the ultimate self — beyond everything, beyond reach and comprehension — is what is called the soul. That is true with regard to Christianity, at least. Easterners like the Buddhists and the Hindus say the *atman* is the real self. Many of the people who are interested in the new-thought movement feel that they are going to be in touch with a higher state of consciousness. They believe that there is an inner state of consciousness that can be touched, which they call their real self, their true self, or their true individuality. And they think that by studying various methods of meditation and changing their lifestyles they will be able to raise their consciousness and touch this immortal part of themselves.

G: Or expand their consciousness.

A: Does this idea have any validity? Is there such a thing as a so-called eternal, higher self which can be touched and brought into the picture? Or is it only human consciousness, or different frequencies of human consciousness, that is being tuned into?

G: What do you think: Is there a higher part of yourself that is in tune with that intelligence?

A: There are obviously many layers within human consciousness. There are many frequencies that could be opened up, if the body and the senses through which we were functioning were expanded through certain meditations, certain ways of living, or certain lifestyles. If these were explored, additional frequencies would probably be open to us and we would become conscious or aware of them. But from my point of view, all of this is a part of human consciousness. The so-called psychic states, for instance, are all a part of human consciousness; they are not separate, they are a part of it. They're a part of what we have put into our consciousness.

G: Are you suggesting there is something beyond?

A: I don't 'know' if there is anything beyond. My feeling is that everything that we can know is part of human consciousness. However, the unknown is outside of human consciousness — the unknown, for instance, of the next moment. There can be an experiencing of the present moment, and in that experiencing, which includes the totality of it, there's an understanding of the present moment. There can be no knowing of the next moment; the future doesn't exist except as an idea.

G: Considering the nature of thought, which we have been discussing, and the whole replay mechanism, how is it possible to touch something that is beyond (if there is anything beyond), something that we can't even name at this point, that which people have named God?

A: Human consciousness is the known, and everything that is within human consciousness is the known.

G: Yes, we've said that many times.

A: You just asked if we can know a higher state, or know God? How can we know it if the known is part of human consciousness? If it is fashioned through time, if it is fragmented, rerun, edited material, it obviously has nothing to do with an eternal reality.

G: No, it can not touch that.

A: It can not touch that eternal reality. You can only know what is already known with the brain and human consciousness. You can delve into known information by means of meditation and certain methods of behavior, or you can raise your level of consciousness so that you are able to perceive other frequencies within the spectrum of consciousness. For instance, some people can see spirits of the dead, or colors of the aura, or the so-called *chakras;* all of these are within human consciousness, but they have nothing to do with the unknown.

They have nothing to do with the moment-to-moment ex-periencing of life.

G: I understand. The implication is that by understanding ourselves we might be able to come to that which is unknown.

A: What is understanding? For instance, as a result of im-personally watching and observing Al over the last forty years in all of his various moods and during all of his various actions, I've come to know that Al is composed of all kinds of things: hereditary tendencies, traits, mannerisms, ways of thinking, lifestyles, prejudices, personal interests, ambitions, fears, loves, and affections. I see that Al is composed of all of these things. I also see that there is nothing eternal in it. There is nothing true in it; there is nothing everlasting in it. It is all very illusory, it is all very fragmented.

When Al dies, when the physical organism comes to an end, it will be the end of all of that material, although a resi-due of it, the essence of it, will probably go into the reservoir of human consciousness, and become part of that. But there is nothing lasting there.

Some of this material may be incarnated again, in another body, but it is not going to be Al that is reincarnated into a new body. It is going to be a part of the residue, the sum total of human consciousness which appears, and which (through a magnetic link with what used to be Al, or the frequency that used to be Al) precipitates itself into a new human being. But that human being will have no memory, or anything to really base any idea of immortality upon.

This, then, is part of knowing myself. When I see that everything I have just described is a fact — and to me it is a fact, since I have watched all of this for forty years — I have no interest in identifying with all that any more. In the beginning, I used to identify with that sort of thing. I had the idea that I would grow through experiences, and that through an evolutionary process, I would become a better person, more spiritual, and so on. But none of these ideas has any permanence, so I have absolutely no interest in identifying with them anymore.

Thus, through negating the things that are not permanent, such as all of my habits and conditioning, an interest has developed in understanding life moment by moment by moment, as it actually occurs. In that there is no idea of continuity. There is no idea of AI continuing at all. There is no idea of 'myself' becoming better and better, and more and more spiritual. There is no idea of being enlightened; there is no idea about anything. There is just a very profound interest in living as factually as possible and responding completely moment by moment.

My own perception of the totality of the moment is limited by the organic structure through which I'm functioning. It is limited by my brain capabilities at the present moment; it is limited by my bodily capacities at the present moment; it is limited by my sensory abilities at the present moment. And these are very individual matters. In other words, what I perceive is obviously confined by certain parameters.

Each person can be absolutely unique if he or she does not use the brain and human consciousness to experience the present moment, for if one is just experiencing, the experiencing will be unique in itself. Obviously, we all experience certain frequencies that are common to all of us. But every person is able to experience uniquely, in his or her own way, and therefore is able to express the results of what life brings in a creative way. In doing this, we touch the otherness which is beyond all thought, that which is the eternal and which can never be known by the brain.

There can be an experiencing, moment by moment, of this otherness, that which we call God, which we call truth. This otherness is beyond anything that the human mind can conceive. The doorway is always there, when the brain and the mind are quiet. In that stillness, there is a possibility of discovering for ourselves that which is eternal.

Wednesday

EXPERIENCING

*Experiencing the totality of the present
moment is the open door through
which insight comes.*

G: Al, to what extent do we learn from experience?

A: Obviously, we learn to do the physical, everyday things of
life. We learn as individuals, but is that learning passed down
through heredity to our children, or to other people? Or does
the memory of that experience and the learning from that
experience remain only with us, and when we die is that the
end of that learning? We have obviously passed down what
we have learned from generation to generation through books,
through the educational system, through the information that
is transmitted from mother to daughter, or from father to
son. But the transmission has to be done directly, in some
physical manner. It is not accomplished by means of an intuitive knowing of what is right and what is wrong, of what to
do or what not to do.

   I think a very good example of this is our response to
war. We obviously have not learned from the countless wars
that have occurred throughout history, because wars have gotten "bigger and better," and more costly in terms of human

47

lives. Much of the technology that we have developed has been directly connected with war and defense. Perhaps technological progress has blinded us to the horrors of war. It has now reached a point where the possibility exists for a nuclear holocaust in which everybody will participate, even though we did not personally instigate it. We are going to participate in it through exposure to deadly radiation, or through being incinerated, or in some other way. We obviously have not passed on a particularly vital piece of information.

On the other hand, we see that animals and the rest of the natural order of life have passed down the results of their experiences to following generations. They are born with that inherent knowledge.

What is the difference between ourselves and other creatures? Why do animals obviously learn from experiencing, while we do not? What is the difference between an experience and experiencing? What do we call an experience, and what do we call experiencing?

G: It seems to me that an experience is something that occurred in the past; you look back and say, "I experienced that." But experiencing exists in the moment.

A: Experiencing always exists in the moment. An experience is something that took place in the past, and which we look back upon; it is part of our memory. We also think that listening to somebody else's experience will enable us to meet future challenges. We obviously pattern our lives in this way, and program ourselves to experience what someone else has experienced, or says he has experienced. We try to pattern our lives after the example of others, hoping to attain the same goals they claim to have attained.

The Buddha had certain experiences in reaching enlightenment under the Bodhi tree, Krishnamurti had certain experiences which led to his fulfillment, and others have apparently accomplished similar things. Therefore, we conceive the idea that we want to attain the state that they attained, or said they attained. We think that by imitating their way of life, or using the particular methods they employed at the time that this happened to them, we can reach the same psychological state.

Can you experience a particular psychological state by imitating somebody else's behavior or somebody else's methods? You can obviously imitate another person's ability to do something physical, like driving an automobile, by imitating their actions. If you want to be able to program a computer the way someone else does, you can learn the necessary procedure; you can study the methods involved and attain the same ability. But can you reach a particular psychological state by imitating methods used by someone else? Aren't the two situations quite distinct?

G: Apparently they are; the world is not filled with Christlike, Buddha-like, or Krishnamurti-like people.

A: That is certainly true! So I think that we should explore the topic of experiencing, which is fairly easy to do because we agreed previously that experiencing is a happening in the moment. From my point of view, experiencing something completely involves total participation in it at any given moment of time. Being fully, completely, consciously aware or awake, giving full attention to whatever is happening at the moment — this is what we can call an experiencing of the moment. I think that we can both agree on that.

49

G: Yes, it is your state of 'now-consciousness.'

A: Yes, using my terminology, it would be the state of now-consciousness; a total participation, through all of your senses, in whatever is happening at a particular moment. Being a participant gives you a feeling of oneness, and an understanding of that moment. You can't pass that on to anyone else. I can't experience a particular moment and convey that experiencing to anyone else. I can write about it, but what I write about isn't the experiencing, because you can not pass the experiencing on. This is obvious, because it is gone; each second, moment by moment by moment, is gone. The next moment it is gone, and it is no longer the experiencing itself.

What we pass on is what we call experience. What we are doing is replaying in our minds what we remember about the experiencing. A description of an event is very similar to a photograph. A camera can only capture a certain limited image, it can only record those things that are directly in front of the lens when the shutter is opened. It can't record something behind the camera, or to the side; it can only capture what is directly in front of it. Obviously, your perception through the camera lens is limited to a small fraction of the total reality of the situation, which involves everything. It involves what is behind the camera and in all directions, as well as everything that can be perceived by both the senses and one's intangible, intuitive ability to apprehend what exists in the totality of the moment. But the camera isn't able to capture that, because the camera is a mechanical thing; the camera was put together through time, so it is limited.

The brain seems to have similar limitations. In order to relate an experience, the brain has to be used; human consciousness has to be used. Human consciousness is the source of the material which is used by the brain; it provides the capacity to analyze situations. It supplies all of the names for the experiences that you are trying to describe. In a way, the brain is just as mechanical as a camera. It is limited in the same way, because it has also been constructed through a linear, evolutionary process of time. Human consciousness is limited because it is composed of everything that anyone has ever put into it through time. All of the experiences that I've related, or that I remember as having happened to me, go into the sum total of human consciousness. We don't know whether these experiences are filtered into it continuously, or whether they become a part of the mass after the physical death of the body, but we know that human consciousness is made up of all this material.

Suppose I have an experience, and I relate my experience to you. I am actually relating a replay of what I remember as having happened, which is limited. It is limited by my brain, my conditioning, my biases, by how I feel about life, by my background, and by my heredity; the entire 'experience' is limited. But that is what is passed on to you, and that is also what passes into human consciousness; it is a sum total of everyone's contributions through probably millions of years.

So this is what we call human experience. All of the books that are in libraries or in universities, all of the knowledge that we transmit, and everything that we consider a part of the educational system, comprise the memories of humanity's experiences. All of it comes out of human consciousness. None of it has anything to do with experiencing, which is multi-dimensional. Knowledge, or memory or experiences, is always two-dimensional, like a photograph.

G: So you are saying that there is personal experience, what-ever I remember about my life over a certain number of years, and there is the memory of experiences present in the consciousness of all of humanity. When you ask whether humanity has learned from the past, the answer apparently is no. On the other hand, if one lives in an intuitive state, or tunes into that knowledge of mankind with a quiet mind, the information is there. Action can be immediately based upon that information, so in that sense there is learning.

A: From my point of view, *you* can not tune into the quiet mind, because when the mind is still, there is no 'you' involved. It can happen, but you can't consciously make it happen. Tuning into the sum total of consciousness does not lead to a quiet mind. It is simply an extension of human consciousness. it is not a part of perception in the present moment.

G: No, I said tuning in with a quiet mind.

A: I disagree.

G: All right. But intuitive knowledge, or the knowledge that is in human consciousness, is intuitively available to someone who is in a quiet state of mind.

A: You are using the term 'quiet mind' in a different way than I do. I'm using the term to refer to something that only occurs in each present moment. You're referring to tuning into the sum total of human experience.

G: I'm referring to more than that. In a state of having a quiet mind there can be an immediate knowing, out of which can come immediate action. Does that knowing come from what humanity has learned before? Does it come from universal consciousness?

A: I don't know. Our human consciousness, as I see it, is the result of all of the edited material, all of the remembered material, all of the knowledge that human beings have accumulated over the ages. This known material can probably be tapped on various levels. Is there another factor there? Does a universal mind exist, which is behind all of the order that we are able to perceive? If so, I don't think that we have any communication with it. There may be some higher type of intuitive knowing available to us, when the personal mind is free of the known; the known, in this case, is what we call the content of consciousness.

That is part of the content. Human consciousness also contains material related to our gaining ascendency over nature. I would consider all occult phenomena to be part of this; all of the occult tradition is part of this, all magic, all of the ceremonial rites which are practiced in the churches and in the different religious establishments. Anything that is used to achieve a certain result which would not be achieved otherwise is part of it. For instance, you may use a pendulum to gain knowledge about certain situations and conditions, in the same way that a doctor may use a thermometer to ascertain whether a patient has a fever or not. The ability to do this, the original idea of doing it, as well as the goals that can be obtained by doing it, are all part of human consciousness.

G: Yes, I understand.

A: But there may exist a universal mind that is distinct from that. It is behind the rotation of the earth, the positions that the planets maintain in relationship to other planets and stars. It governs the flight of birds from one area to another during different seasons. It maintains an absolute order in which we participate, even though we consider ourselves unique. We are actually a part of this order, even though at present we are doing our best to separate ourselves from it. We are doing our best to scramble around and mess it up. But we are really part of it, because everything that we see in the world is part of this universal creation and part of the universal mind, which is completely impersonal; it doesn't care about personalities. It doesn't care about you getting a good job, or getting more money, or anything else.

So there are two distinct types of consciousness, aren't there? One of these is the universal mind, which is completely impersonal, which can not be manipulated by us, or by anything that we can think about it. If you want to experience it, to experience the peace and quiet and tranquility which is part of it, then you have to live the kind of a life that will bring your mental 'frequency' into accordance or harmony with that universal consciousness, that universal mind. It is not going to accommodate to you; you are going to have to accommodate to it.

G: Are you saying that it is entirely separate from human consciousness, or what human experience has put into consciousness?

A: I feel that it is completely separate.

G: Then where does true learning come in? Can you learn at all, other than physical technological things, from this storehouse of human experience? Or does true learning — growth, understanding, change — all emerge from having a quiet mind, from intuition, from what you are calling the universal mind?

A: Obviously anything that is a part of human consciousness can be learned. You can learn to participate in a religious ceremony. You can learn to meditate in a certain way. You can learn to drive an automobile, or you can learn to fly.

G: Or go to the moon.

A: You can learn to use all of the different techniques that humanity has learned. But they are all a part of human consciousness, which is not a part of what I call the universal mind. The things that you learn individually, through those methods, will not be passed down to your offspring. If you have a son or daughter, he or she will not be born with the ability that you have acquired. This seems to be the problem with human beings.

We have been going along like this for thousands of years, and we still have not learned some very basic, fundamental things. We are not born with the capacity to avoid war. We are not born with the capacity to see the true values in life. We haven't learned any of this. However, as I said in the very beginning, the animals and all of the natural creatures seem to learn it.

In 1925, when I first drove from Ohio to California, I counted 250 dead animals on the road in one day. Today, if I went back through the same area, I probably would not see a single dead animal on that road. The animals have learned not to go out on the road; they have learned to be wary of automobiles. They do not just wander around, randomly. They have learned from direct experiencing not to do that, and that kind of learning is different.

We are not doing that. Instead of meeting each moment factually, we meet each moment with ideas derived from human consciousness. The ideas, images about how to react to a particular kind of experience, consist of information that has been passed from generation to generation, through education and through tradition. Meeting a situation with an idea, as I said before, is very similar to viewing a situation in terms of a photograph; all we see is the photograph. We don't see what is really happening; we're watching the photograph. Since the experience is only two-dimensional, it is not handed down to us through heredity.

This, I think is the great difference between the two states: We can have access to the information and the intelligence that is available to us through the universal mind, or we can be cut off from that source because of our ideas, and only function in terms of the information available to us within human consciousness.

From my point of view, true learning is a result of experiencing completely, moment by moment, as you are living your life in a state of now-consciousness, awareness, or complete attention. There is a learning in that which will be passed down through succeeding generations, because it will go into, and will become part of, the universal mind.

Therefore, don't we really have access to two possible sources of information upon which to base our lives and our living, as well as two possible ways to use these sources? One of these ways is the well-known method that everybody is using, which involves relying upon the information within human consciousness. However, the possibility exists that we may see how limited that is, how fragmentary that is, how it can never really be creative; it can never supply information that is completely applicable to a momentary happening. Traditional information is necessary to deal with all of the different kinds of physical, phenomenal things that happen in life, and we use it in that way. We use the brain to interpret, or supply, this material. We learn to do different things. But to see its limits, to see to what extent it can be used, and to see where it falls short in providing totally appropriate responses at any given moment, is essential. We always have an approximate behavioral pattern available that we can follow, because we act according to an image or an idea. The essence of these fragmented experiences becomes a part of the reservoir of human consciousness; however, universal mind can only accept the essence of complete experiencing. Do you understand what I'm trying to say?

G: Yes, exactly. And the more humanity contributes to this personal consciousness and relies upon it, the less chance there is for fundamental change.

A: Human consciousness doesn't change. You can add to it interminably, which is what has been done through the centuries, we are always adding to it, we are always gaining so-called 'new' experiences. This is what is considered progress.

G: And we are stuffing computers full of it.

A: Yes, and we are living in accordance with the computer. Before the computer was developed, we were living in accordance with tradition. We lived in accordance with the experiences of others down through the ages, experiences passed down through the educational system and so on. But we've now learned an easier way to do it. We now have computers, so we program the computers with all of our information. Instead of a person actually experiencing a situation, he presses a button on a computer, and out comes information; and that is what he patterns his lifestyle upon, readout from a mechanical device.

G: So the computer can create a new religion! But it will

always consist of more and more of what is already known, of what is already present in the consciousness of humanity.

A: A computer can not create something that is unknown, can it? It is only capable of being programmed to produce known information. It can not touch the unknown, and creativity is the unknown.

G: True.

A: Something made by man can be a result of creative thinking, but it is not creation. Creation itself is something that is happening moment by moment, and that is not derived from programmed information.

G: I'm not sure thinking can ever be creative; perhaps it can only be technologically cumulative. So that is the difference; either you are functioning from the known (whether it is your own personal known, or books or computers), or else you are capable of putting all of that aside, of doubting it all and questioning it all, and functioning entirely differently.

A: To be able to use the known when it is necessary, but lay it aside when it is not needed, allows one to perceive directly the holistic nature of the present moment.

G: That moment includes beauty, love, feeling, order, everything in fact that one needs. But you can see what a revolutionary idea we are discussing — the putting aside of all of what we know, and have stuffed into our computers and libraries!

A: And the tricky part is that you can not consciously put

this material aside. You can not say, "Well, I'm going to put aside human knowledge, I'm going to put aside everything that I think about or know." You can not consciously do that, because it is just another expression of human consciousness. It is like sitting down to meditate with a purpose in mind.

G: I see.

A: It is all part of the same thing; the only way it can be approached is negatively. The possibility exists that we can become aware of the fact that we are using old material instead of looking at something with new eyes. We can discover the limits of the usual approach through experiments with ourselves, through study, and through false ideas about meditation. We can go through all of that, and by trying it all, reach a point where we may suddenly wake up to the fact that we have been involved in the thinking mechanism. And at that moment of awareness, reality is suddenly staring us in the face. There is the present moment with all its beauty, all of its millions of bits of information, all of its open channels, and we are not involved in it at all. We are not seeing it — it is perception itself, which is outside of human consciousness — that is seeing. The body's eyes and senses are being used by perception, but there is no identification with the thought process. The seer and the seen are one!

G: Yes!

A: Thus perception involves something that you have *not* done. As soon as you recognize or identify something you have done, it is gone. Perception has to be a completely non-identified state. This, I feel, is the open doorway to the universal mind, which supplies everything necessary for you to function at a particular moment in a logical, sane, and complete manner.

When you are in this impersonal state, there is never a question about what to do. If somebody presents you with a challenge, you will respond to that challenge in a sane, logical way. But you can not use perception ahead of time, and you can not use it to edit material that has already been put into your personal computer. It is completely inviolable; you can not violate it in any way. You can not exploit it, or gain something personally from it.

G: There is no motive, no goal to be achieved.

A: There is no goal or any other end that you can think of; it can not be used for any of that.

G: So this sets aside all psychological experience, all 'knowledge' about yourself, and places you beyond conditioning, so that you are not thinking in patterns, or reacting. Again, this sounds tremendously revolutionary. How does one come to this?

A: Perhaps by trying all of the known escapes.

G: People have been doing that for a very long time.

A: It takes a lot of ground clearing, a lot of clearing away the brush. It requires a running down of false leads, false ideas, and false escapes, trying this thing or that thing, trying meditation, torturing oneself, trying all of the things that people have attempted in order to achieve this state. But they have seldom achieved it. They have never achieved it through any

60

traditional, self-centered method or technique. It has come, but it has come 'like a thief in the night,' unexpectedly, unannounced, when all barriers are down.

G: Through the back door.

A: The back door was suddenly open because something apparently short-circuited access to human consciousness. It was bypassed, possibly because of a shock or a sudden bereavement, or because the person was suddenly denuded of an idea which had been uppermost in his mind, and which had been influencing his actions and ideas for a long time. Suddenly the idea was taken away from him, and in that vacuum the door was open. The cup was suddenly empty, and since 'nature abhors a vacuum,' universal intelligence flowed into that opening, and was immediately there.

G: So the mind has to be absolutely quiet, and there are various ways that this might occur. First, of course, there has to be a willingness, an inner intention for the door to open. But you are also saying that you have to have reached a state in which you tell yourself, "I don't know." Perhaps you have become so frustrated that you can not think your way into quietness, or you can not think anymore about the problem, or you have done all of the thinking that you can and have slept on it overnight. Whatever the reason, the mind is in a state where it is completely puzzled. There are no answers anymore. It reminds me of the story of the Zen master who hits his pupil over the head with a stick when he fails to answer an impossible riddle; the moral of the story is that the sequence of events may possibly create a vacuum into which truth can flow.

A: In order for an insight to come, or for enlightenment to occur, I think it is necessary for us to stretch our human capacities to the utmost. We have to learn to think clearly; we have to learn to think logically; we have to be willing to explore all avenues. We have to be willing to look into all possibilities, and when this is done, then creativity or the capacity for insight is the next step. I don't think that insight, or the state of having a quiet mind, will come to someone who is lazy, unwilling to look into things, unwilling to find out about himself, or unwilling to experiment.

Take great scientists, or musicians, or any other people who have creative insight and who are actually creating something new. They have developed their art to the utmost of their capability; they have learned the technique involved. In other words, technique is necessary; the technique of thinking clearly, the technique of evaluating impersonally what comes up in life. All of that is just as much of a technique as a musician's skills. When you have developed your technique as far as your individual capabilities allow, insight is the next logical step, because you have pushed your capabilities to their limits. You have done everything you possibly can and then because you can not think of anything you have not done, there is a quiet space. And that *is* quietness, isn't it? If you've really done it, then this is the place, this is the jumping-off spot. There is a vacuum at that time; and into that vacuum, into that empty cup, comes insight.

The insight you have at that moment can be used by the brain, and by human consciousness, for further development. You progress as far as you can go in a certain direction, and then there is the quietness, because you don't know where else to go. Suddenly insight comes again, and with it comes the capacity to carry that insight further. Life has thrown the ball to you; you grab the ball and run with it some more, until you have completed that particular move. Then perhaps another opening occurs, another vacuum, and life again throws you the ball, and you run with it still further.

If you are living a creative life, this is what is happening. But if you are clinging to a technique and are satisfied with that technique, you are stuck with it; the opening never occurs. You never experience the vacuum through which life can offer you these creative opportunities. You never come to the open door of the present moment.

G: Yes, that sounds very true. Perhaps something happens to the brain itself when you set aside psychological experiences and meet challenges freshly.

A: I think that what we call normal human behavior is very limited; certainly the things that most people are interested in are very limited. People are limited by their background, they are limited by their prejudices, and they are limited by the society in which they've grown up; all of these things are limiting. The fragments of life that we identify with, out of all of the experiences that occur to us, only require the use of a certain portion of our brain cells. It has been said that we only use ten percent of the capacity of our brain because it only takes ten percent to respond to the narrow requirements of any particular lifestyle. However, experiencing the totality of any given moment — which is now-consciousness — would obviously require the activation of many new brain cells.

We then find that we are flowing freely with the evolutionary life force. When we have given up all self-centered activity there is true psychological security.

THE QUIET MIND

*Meditation is renewal, a dying each day
to the past. It is an intense passive
awareness; a burning away of the
desire to continue the known, the
desire to become the more.*

G: What I want to ask is this: Can one do anything to achieve
the state of a quiet mind? People talk a great deal about quiet
minds, and silence; they go to retreats for meditation, they go
an entire weekend without talking. These actions may create
an atmosphere, but can thought stop itself? Can one do anything to be quiet, or does it come about in another way?
One's mind chatters constantly even when one is trying to
sleep. In a dozing condition the mind chatters, and this produces dreams. Then you wake up and realize that your mind
has gone over the previous day, or what you're going to do
when you get up. So I suppose the question is this: Can
thought stop itself, or does a state of quietness come about in
an entirely different way?

A: Can thought stop itself?

G: I'm not sure; I don't think it can, but I'm not sure.

A: Isn't thought stopping itself just another facet of the same thinking process? If so, then thought isn't really stopping itself; it can train itself to do different things, but it is still following the same pattern.

G: I know that; but still the mind says, thought says, "Let's stop all of this extraneous, repetitive thinking process. Let's do something different." So thought is considering the idea of being quiet. Thought is saying: "Perhaps if I'm quiet enough, insight will come, space will come, timelessness will come." I think it is my mind, my brain, thought itself saying, "How can I be silent?"

A: I don't know; I don't know about a chattering mind, because my mind doesn't chatter. My mind is quiet most of the time; not for long periods of time, but on an intermittent basis. It is a condition of being in and out of perception, in and out of attention. But in a state of observation, when you're really observing something, or are interested in something, is your mind chattering?

G: No; if I'm totally perceptive, then the chattering stops. If I'm totally perceptive, then there is no thinking. When I'm totally perceptive, there is a possibility of insight occurring. But then something says, "I want more of that." Something in my memory says, "I should get back to that. I shouldn't chatter, I shouldn't think; I should use thought when I need to during the day, and then let the brain rest." So all of that occurs. There is the memory of the silent perception, the state in which insights come. So perhaps the question is this: Can I *do* anything? Many people take time to sit down and meditate or try to be quiet; they watch thought, and try to follow it through to its end. But when you're concerned with thought, there is no end to it. So can you do anything to be quiet?

A: I don't think so, although I can only speak from my own experience, which (as you know) started a long time ago. But can thought be quiet if you have any motive, if you have any goal in mind, if you have something that you want, if you have any choice; can the mind be quiet under any of those circumstances?

G: No, I don't think so, because I've observed that if I think, "I'll sit down and be quiet and meditate so that maybe I'll go into a very quiet state and have an insight," nothing happens. It is like going out for a walk and looking at the sunset and saying, "Now I want a marvelous experience." Thought is involved in that, and so it still exists in time.

A: I think that it probably takes a lot of groundwork to reach the state of having a quiet mind. Although no method is involved, I do think certain prerequisites are necessary; at least they seem to be. One prerequisite is this: I have to have seen very, very clearly that anything I do as an ego, or achieve as a goal that I have set for myself, is just part of the same rat-race; it is part of the rearrangement of human consciousness. But most of us haven't realized that yet; we think that it is possible to rearrange the pieces to our satisfaction, so that we can get by. Obviously, we can rearrange them to some extent. But life is always presenting us with events which we can't foresee ahead of time. And all of our planning and our little schemes come to nothing; we have a stroke, or we have an accident, or somebody dies, or somebody leaves us; there is always something happening. So I don't think there is any answer within the field of human consciousness. If you see that very clearly, then I think you can have the inner intention to wake up every time you identify with that sort of thing and it will begin to occur.

That is one prerequisite. Another prerequisite would be not wanting anything. And that takes a lot of doing, because everybody wants something. They want a quiet mind, or they want peace, or they want an automobile; they want something; it is all there like a great department store. And you can have almost anything you want if you are willing to wait long enough for it.

G: So to sit down to meditate and say, "I want a state of quietness," is the wrong approach.

A: You can achieve a false state of quietness. You can achieve the generally accepted idea of what a state of quietness is by doing different things. Certain meditations can produce an artificial state of quietness. But it is an enforced state, and it only lasts as long as you're in the particular environment in which you can produce it. Some people have a certain room in which they sit and meditate, while other people have a particular location, or tree, or whatever. They go through a certain procedure to arrive at an artificial state of quietness. But the moment that they are taken away from that environment, or they have to go back to work, or go back to town, or whatever, it is gone. So it is not a lasting state.

G: And it doesn't work in their daily life.

A: It doesn't work in their daily life because it is not complete; it is two dimensional. It is like having a photograph of a quiet state of mind, and then imagining yourself in that state. It isn't complete.

G: Yes. I've observed that that is not what is happening in your case. I've noticed that one of the things that you do is to not allow yourself to think more than you need to about something. The first thing you do if a challenge or a question comes up is to be quiet. I suppose you're just looking at that question, that challenge. Then if there is any thinking to be done about it, you do it, but very briefly. And then you're quiet again; you pause, and you let it go. If someone says, "Well, don't you think we should work this out," very often you'll say, "I don't want to think about it today; I'll think about it when the time comes. I don't want to chew it like a dog with a bone."

It seems to me that it is a conscious act when you say, "I'm not going to think about this any further," and you go into a quiet waiting. Perhaps what you are doing is observing. It seems to me that you go into a preliminary state of consciously putting thought aside; perhaps at first you observe it. It seems to me that you wait, and you just stay with the question. Then you receive an insight and come up with the right answer to the challenge. This comes from observing you, living with you; that is what you seem to do. You may think briefly about a problem, and then you consciously say, "I'm not going to think about it any more," and you stay with the question.

A: The challenge comes and I take the first step. There is an instant perception that it is a challenge, and an instant perception that I'm faced with something new. And that is the last step, because again there is an instantaneous perception or insight as to whether or not it is an immediate challenge. If it is, then the next step is to take action. I see something burning and immediately I act, or I am suddenly confronted with a rattlesnake, or whatever, and I immediately take action. There is no thinking involved in the action, there is just doing.

But my original perception might be that the problem is not immediate, that it involves something that is coming up in the future. For example, sometimes you will try to embroil me in something, or try to get me to think about something, that you feel must be considered at once although it is going to have to be done in the future. But I won't concern myself with it because to me it is not an immediate problem. Things are going to change, in fact they may change radically, but when the time comes to really act, I'll know exactly what to do. So I don't want to think about a situation ahead of time.

G: Yes, that's putting thought aside.

A: So I do use thought. If I want to plan something ahead of time, I obviously have to use thought.

G: To prepare, yes.

A: There is a right time to plan. For instance, if we decided that we wanted to go to Europe next July, Sunday obviously would not be the day to do anything about it. We shouldn't even think about it. If we still wanted to go to Europe at 10:00 on Monday morning, the next step would be to contact the travel agency and obtain the facts.

G: Yes.

A: That would be the next step. Then, as soon as that was finished, we should drop it. We should not think about it anymore.

G: Yes, I understand that about physical things, but let us stay with psychological matters.

70

A: I don't let psychological matters hang on. I try to finish them as soon as they arise. If a situation involves someone that I have a psychological problem with, I can't wait until I go to see that person to talk to them about it.

G: Yes.

A: But that is not what most thought is concerned with. The question is, what are the prerequisites for a quiet mind? One of them definitely is to see that anything that I do in the way of controlling thought, or rearranging the ideas to represent what I want them to represent, does not lead to a quiet mind. I must realize that anything like that that I do just postpones the problem.

G: But you have this marvelous way of just putting thought aside when there is a question or a challenge. If someone questions you and pushes you, then you might bring up a memory or a story, or describe the way something worked in the past. But if somebody really challenges you with something important, I've noticed that you don't think about it at all; you stay very quietly with the question. Are you consciously putting thought aside, or do you just drop it?

A: It just drops away. The minute that there is a perception of what the challenge entails, there is a perception as to whether or not it requires thought at that moment. When you see the fallacy of something, you don't have to push it aside; it just drops away. If you see the fallacy of a certain action, really see it, in that moment there is a perception or right action. You don't have to think about it.

G: All right, so you don't consciously put thought aside.

71

A: No, it just drops away on its own. It withers away.

G: Thought has no place in the perception.

A: It has no place in complete perception of the present moment.

G: Right; if you stay with the question, and observe the question as if it is brand new and you have never talked about that challenge, that question before, there is no place for thought at all.

A: There is a time to use thought, and a time not to use it. It should not be used if the challenge requires action in the future.

G: Yes. So we've established that you can't think your way into quietness.

A: No. Can you really see that that is a fact? You can think yourself into artificial quietness, man-made quietness; you can obviously do that. That's what all of the systems of medi-tation do. But that isn't really quietness; the moment you leave that particular context the whole thing blows up, and you're back in the rat-race, fighting with your wife, or whatever. But real quiet doesn't depend on your location or what your oc-cupation happens to be.

G: Let us explore this a moment longer, because people go through all of these steps in order to be quiet; this is called meditation. Now they are bringing it into Yoga. I noticed that an entire recent issue of the *Yoga Journal* was concerned with this subject; it stated that if you do Yoga, Yoga is only a first step in becoming enlightened. People are using Floatation Tanks and meditation music tapes are selling like hotcakes. People are creating all of these atmospheres in order to be quiet. Obviously, if you want to go to sleep at night and your mind keeps saying, "I wish I had said that," and "I must write that letter tomorrow," and "Why didn't I do so and so," and "I" should do such an such," you're not going to go to sleep. So I think the point comes where you consciously go through all of that daily stuff, and either tell your mind to postpone it or set it aside, because you can't do anything about it tonight. As you said before, if you want tickets to travel on Sunday, you have to wait until Monday anyway, so why think about it? So in that sense, you consciously put thought away and say, "I'm not going to think about all of that stuff now, I am here to meditate." This is what people are doing; they go through all sorts of things — physically, emotionally, and mentally — to have a quiet mind. That may be a first step, but then what?

A: What happens when you wake up in the middle of the night, or when you're quiet, and realize that someone had called you earlier and had wanted you to call back, and you had promised that you would but had forgotten to do it? Is that kind of material part of the chattering mind?

G: That's what I mean by a chattering mind: "I wish I had, why didn't I, I should," et cetera.

A: So if you realize this, and your real inner intention is to have a quiet mind, you pick up the telephone and call the person back at the first opportunity. What happens then to that particular memory? Is it still there in the chatter, or is it gone?

G: It is gone, because you've taken care of it.

A: Then why can't you do that with everything that is unfinished? What that really means is that you have to become aware of what the mind is chattering about. That's the first step.

G: You have to be aware all day long, not just half an hour here or there.

A: All of the time, moment by moment.

G: Right.

A: So you have to find out what the mind chatters about. That's what I did forty years ago; I began with that. My mind was chattering about Latin America, and the tropics, and many other things. One by one I took care of them, just as one would call a person or write a letter.

G: Yes, I see.

A: And I was very careful that I didn't occupy my mind with other activities to take the place of the ones that were eliminated.

G: Don't keep yourself busy with new activities, so that you create more clutter to leave unfinished.

A: Whether that clutter is meditation or something else. Meditation can become a 'bucket-filling' activity just like anything else; the only difference is that the word meditation has positive connotations for many people; it makes you more spiritual, and so on. But it is as much a method of filling the mind as playing cards, or any other type of mind-game that people indulge in, is.

G: So you are saying that you keep order in your life.

A: That's right. The perception of disorder leads naturally to true order.

G: You make order as you go along, all day long.

A: You do all of the 'homework' that you've been given, and you finish all of the things that you've committed yourself to do.

G: And if you can't do them immediately, you realize that they can not be done until tomorrow, or next week, and that realization also quiets the mind.

A: That's right. And if a person to whom you have an obligation isn't available, let it go because you can't do anything about it. And each time that something like that drops away, be awake so that you don't fill that space with some other type of mental activity; just leave it alone. And slowly, imperceptibly the mind quiets, because the moment something is gone there is space.

G: In most people the space is very brief, because there is something about thought, there is something about our whole conditioning, that causes us to think that it is important to be always doing something. We don't seem to think (or we have never been told) that it is important to be quiet, and we don't raise our children to see its importance either. So habit is part of it, conditioning is part of it. Even when you have nothing to do, thought says, "I should feed the birds; I should prepare for the next meal; I should call so-and-so, I haven't talked to them for ages" — do anything except sit quietly. That's something else one has to realize.

A: Also, it can probably be downright scary not to have something happening all of the time.

G: For most people, yes. They say, "I'm bored." Kids say it all the time; teenagers say, "I'm bored, there is nothing happening, what will I do?" And parents usually give them something to do: "Here, draw in your book, or go watch TV; don't bother me; I don't know what you want to do, go out and play, but go do something!" Why is it scary?

A: Have you ever watched the animals or birds or other natural creatures, like the cat lying on your lap right now, or your dog? If you observe their activities, you see that there is a time for play; there is a time for being quiet; there is a time for direct action; there is a time for food; there is a time for every function in their life pattern.

G: Yes, of course.

A: But people are different; we each have a 'monkey on our back' that forces us to be constantly thinking. We have to be busy all the time, because we've cut ourselves off from nature, we've cut ourselves off from the normal, natural way of living, and we instinctively know that we're on our own. Every time that you're thinking in a self-centered way, everytime that your thought pattern is involved in the thinking process, you know inwardly that you're on your own; you know that you're paddling your own canoe. There is a feeling of insecurity, a feeling that "I've got to keep going, I've got to keep moving, I mustn't relax; I mustn't let down at all."

You know, it is a result of a lack of faith, isn't it? I think the animals and the birds, and every other living thing live in a state of faith; real, true faith. They don't do it consciously; they aren't saying, "I have faith in life," but they live in a state of faith. And we, because of our thinking, don't live in a state of true faith. We don't feel that we are an integral part of the natural order of life, so at the deep level where faith is born, we are really lonely. Our self-centered way of life has cut us off from an intuitive feeling of unity with life.

G: That's where the fear comes in: to be alone, to be quiet, to face things by ourselves. We've been taught to go out and either do things like somebody else — the hero or the authority — or to talk things over with our psychiatrist or our priest or our best friend. But nobody ever says, "Deal with it alone, and see what happens." That is where the fear comes in.

A: You see, the difficulty in going into any of these life problems is that everything is interconnected. And the only thing that we can do when we discuss something is to take it step by step in a linear way and think about it.

G: I don't feel that we are thinking about it now, we are just observing it.

A: Shouldn't one of our first tasks be to ask ourselves why we are even discussing a quiet mind? Why have a quiet mind? There would be all kinds of answers to that. Perhaps we've read that if one has a quiet mind something good will happen.

Or perhaps we want a quiet mind because it is very inconvenient to have a mind that is chattering all of the time; if one wakes up in the middle of the night and the mind is chattering then one can't go to sleep. That would be a very practical reason to have a quiet mind.

G: No, I wasn't asking for those reasons.

A: Has thought itself seen the futility of its own chattering? Or is a quiet mind just an idea that we have acquired through reading a book or hearing somebody else talking, or through some means like that?

G: For most people it is an idea; it is something to be achieved. But I wasn't asking for that reason either.

A: No, you weren't.

G: I was asking because I've been there, and I would like to get back there more often. Once again, are there specific steps that lead one to a state of quietness?

A: Yes, I think so.

G: We've mentioned certain things, such as order in one's daily life.

A: The only guidelines I have to go by are the events in my own life. Forty years ago there was an ending of ambition. I've had no ambition to do anything since. You've lived with me for 24 years, you should agree with this. Do you see any ambition in me?

G: No, none.

A: None at all; I really don't have any ambition. If you have an ambition, then fear is an inevitable corollary.

G: Yes, the fear of not achieving it.

A: Yes. So fear keeps the mind busy, chattering. Ambition keeps the mind chattering; wanting something other than 'what is' keeps the mind chattering; dreaming up pictures of the future keeps the mind chattering; even thinking about how cute little Lhasa Apso puppies are keeps the mind chattering!

G: Earlier you referred to something new; you talked about staying with 'what is.' That's very important. But staying with 'what is' can also occupy your mind or your thoughts a great deal. Do you know what I mean? Some people misinterpret the whole meaning of staying with 'what is.' We know some people who seriously feel that they are doing what Krishnaji is talking about. They say that they are constantly busy with 'what is,' and they totally occupy their minds, their brains, and their thought patterns all day long with what they refer to as 'what is.' But to me, all they seem to be doing is living in a very self-centered state in relationship to other people. They are concerned totally with themselves, in a very self-centered way, rather than in a way that might lead to self-understanding. They excuse this by saying, "I have to stay with myself," and so they become rather peculiar people. It is not a valid occupation! It is not a carte blanche to do and be anything you want to be, and to heck with everybody else.

A: Perhaps we can approach this question about the quiet

mind a little differently. Logically, we can see that this present moment, *now,* contains a thousand different bits and pieces of information. There are many bits of information right here in front of us, in the room; look at the cat, for example, and the fact that she just looked out of the window and then turned around the other way, which shows that there was something outside. All of that is here; and there is also a feeling between you and I, and a feeling between you and I and the cat and the dog; there is a feeling about the whole situation. In other words, the entire experience is available to us, but it is only available when we are in a state of observation. In a state of observation the mind is quiet. The minute the mind identifies with any of the bits of information available, then it isn't quiet, because it is going off on a tangent and identifying with one little segment of the reality of the moment.

G: It can select any one thing: the dog, the cat, the bird, or any idea which is a response to memory.

A: So couldn't that be a proper incentive for desiring — or rather having the inner intention to have — a quiet mind? I see that each moment contains all of this information, includes everything, everything that my five senses can take in and absorb, as well as intangible things that I can only feel and sense intuitively. It contains all of that. In seeing that totality, and in seeing it in the very moment of observation, this moment *now,* there is no future, there is no time involved; there is no problem in what to do, I don't have to think about it at all. In fact, the moment I think about it, I have identified with one segment of it, and taken off with it, and I'm not aware of all of the rest. To see that as a fact, to really experience it, to me is a true incentive for desiring a quiet mind.

This eliminates all ambition or desire to do this or that, or thought of gain. Because at the moment of observation there is no thought of gain. The moment is complete; I'm in it, I'm part of it, I can't even think about gain. I can think about gaining something, but then I'm not into the moment anymore. The minute I think about gaining something out of this present moment, I've identified with one segment of it. There is understanding, love, and affection; in fact, all of the so-called virtues are already present in this particular moment. There can be no question about what to do with the present moment. To see that, and to experience that, is to be the real incentive for desiring a quiet mind.

If you do see it, you're no longer satisfied with the old approach anymore; you have to begin anew. You have to begin to wake up and become conscious of what your mind is occupied with. And one by one, you have to finish this particular problem, that particular piece of homework — your letter or whatever it might be. It then drops away; you don't have to drop it.

G: What do you mean by perceiving the moment? That is a very interesting way of putting it.

A: I mean giving full attention to the moment, completely observing the moment.

G: This moment you and I are sitting here quietly. I question anything that comes up. That is what is happening with me. Anything that comes up, I just let drop. If something comes up from my memory, from the past, or if something comes up concerning what we could do an hour from now, such as lunch or whatever, I just let it go.

A: You don't let it go; perception finishes it.

G: No, I don't give it energy, I don't give it attention.

A: Isn't the thought process constantly being rejected when intelligence sees that it isn't necessary at any particular moment?

G: Yes; I didn't want to use that word, rejection, but I think you're right. I don't consciously say that I'm not going to think about something; I just drop it.

A: The minute perception catches you thinking about something, it is gone. There is no rejection, there is no dropping; it is gone, it disappeares. But the next moment it may come back, because of the thought habits of the mind.

G: Well, you talked about all of the thousands of bits of information that surround us, both tangible and intangible, and which comprise our memory, our thoughts of the future. We can sit here and imagine all kinds of things, and waste an hour. So what is happening right now is that you and I are consciously — I say dropping it or laying it aside, you say rejecting it — pushing this material aside, letting it go. I was going to say that whatever comes up that doesn't seem important in this moment I'm putting aside, but that is choice.

A: In discussing this, I have to use the thought process in order to communicate. But if you are sitting there quietly and not speaking, if you are listening with complete attention, then the thought process is bypassed and there is direct perception leading to holistic understanding. If you see the fallacy in thinking about something ahead of time when it isn't necessary, you only have to catch yourself when you're doing it. Catch yourself when you're not attentive. Catch yourself thinking, because awareness and thought can't take place at the same time.

Suppose you've identified with a particular train of thought for a certain length of time, and suddenly you become conscious that you've been doing this. In that moment of awareness, there can be a perception of how identifying with that thought has obviously kept you from experiencing all of the other things that have been going on around you during that particular period of time. In perceiving that, it drops away. But you can then identify with something else; that's the problem. The interface between awareness and thought is so fleeting.

G: It drops away, that's right. So you aren't constantly rejecting, or judging, or saying I won't think about that; you just let it go.

A: It withers away.

G: All right, and then what happens?

A: Then you're in a state of pure perception again, aren't you?

G: So this process could go on and on. Is this what you're referring to when you talk about going on and on all day long?

A: Certainly; you're in and out of it all day long. But as you take care of each item, and add no further items to it, you find the periods of quietness becoming longer. The periods of identification with thought come at less frequent intervals, and the fleeting interface between two thoughts becomes the state of the quiet mind.

G: There is something else as well, because you're not just saying that there is silence between two thoughts.

A: There is silence between two thoughts, isn't there?

G: But something more happens, something else happens, because everyone has experienced silence between two thoughts. They get up and dress; they think about dressing, and what to wear, and then they're quiet. And then they think about what they are going to have for breakfast, and they're quiet. Then they go to work, and so on.

A: I question whether or not they're quiet in the interim. I think that their minds are chattering on other subjects without their being conscious of it.

G: But I think that what you've described, in a way, is quietness between two thoughts. I think that the state of having a quiet mind, total awareness, encompasses something more, or something different, because when you remain in that state it is so complete that other things don't come up; it takes over, it is there.

A: Well, I don't think about Arabian horses anymore. There was a time when I thought about Arabian horses all of the time.

G: Someone might say that you just got bored with the subject. No, I don't mean that; I mean if thought says something, you drop it. If memory says something, you drop it. If the phone rings, if you have a conversation, you drop it. But you don't spend your day just doing that. I've observed you, and I know that there are times when you are totally in that state of having a quiet mind; where you are totally alone, without fear, without ambition, without anything — or one with everything.

A: As I am right now. My mind is completely quiet in listening to you. Of course, when I'm talking it isn't, obviously.

G: When you're conveying "I am," of course you're out of that state. But I've observed that you can be in a state in which the whole room is quiet, if I enter it. It isn't as if you're just between two thoughts. The state I'm talking about creates an atmosphere around you in which the room is quiet, the animals are quiet, and there seems to be a feeling of total harmony. That doesn't mean that you're off on 'cloud nine.' It doesn't mean that if I need to say something to you, you don't respond. But it is more than just a split second of quietness between two thoughts.

A: I think it is the same thing, but it is an expansion of it. In other words, when I first started out 40 years ago, there would be just a fraction of space between two thoughts, in which this quiet existed. But as identification with certain ideas has dropped away, these spaces have become wider and wider, so that at the present time it is as you have described. There is a state of quietness, unless something comes along which suddenly attracts my attention, and I identify with it.
    I feel that anybody can experience this momentary space between two thoughts, provided that their mind is not cluttered up too badly. The more uncluttered it is, the quieter a life they've lived, the more chance there is of catching themselves experiencing the space between two thoughts. The experience may only be momentary, a split second in the beginning, but anybody can have it. Perhaps Krishnaji was born in this state,

so there was this quietness there all the time; maybe, I don't know.

G: We can't talk about him.

A: I wasn't born with a quiet mind, it didn't happen that way. In my case, after 40 years, I've reached a point where I can say that my mind really is quiet; most of the time it is quiet. Once in a while I'll identify with a news report, or state my personal, biased opinion on something, but the minute that I do, I'm aware of it, and I either give into it and voice a great many more opinions to go with it, or I drop it. Sometimes, when I'm tired or don't feel good, I'll just identify with something and go with it; I'll let my conditioning take over, and I'll spout off a lot of nonsense. But if I'm feeling well, and I've had plenty of sleep, and everything is all right, that doesn't happen.

G: When one is quiet it is all very simple, it is all very open.

A: Because the present moment is simple and open, isn't it?

G: And there is no thought, "How did I get here?"

A: That's right.

G: Or, "How will I return?"

A: That's right; at this moment you're not thinking that at all, are you?

G: I'm not thinking.

A: You don't need to use thought in this present moment, except to escape from the present moment. You can escape by using thought, but if you want to stay in the present moment you can't use thought; the minute you use thought you're away from the present moment.

G: Right.

A: It is just that simple.

G: Yes, it is that simple.

A: The important thing is that it actually works; it is a fact of life. And it is so simple that it requires absolutely no method at all. It requires no practice, no technique. In fact, any method that you use, or any technique that you use, takes you away from this present moment, because it is a part of thought.

G: Right, and yet you have pointed out certain things that are prerequisites.

A: Maybe they aren't even prerequisites. Perhaps it isn't important to see that all thought is part of human consciousness. Maybe it isn't a prerequisite, maybe it is just an idea. When Krishnaji was asked, "Why did this come to you, why did this happen to you?" he stated, "Maybe because the cup was empty." Maybe his mind was empty. And maybe the same thing would come to anyone whose mind was quiet and empty.

The mind has the capacity to be quiet, and empty, and fresh, and vulnerable, each and every moment. But we never give ourselves a chance to discover this, because of habit and education and all the other conditioning that we human beings have recieved through the course of millions of years. We don't give ourselves a chance to live in a state of faith like the animals, and the birds, and the trees do. But each moment contains faith. If you don't run off with a thought system and identify with a fragment of the available information, then you are in a state of grace, you're in a state of sacredness, you're in a state of faith.

You've got the whole stream of life flowing by. Everyone is paddling around in the stream of life, paddling in a chosen direction. You are bucking the stream, you're fighting the current. But you might suddenly become aware of the fact that all of your activities in the stream of life, in the way of paddling around, have been completely useless as far as taking you toward the true reality of life is concerned. Paddling around can take you to fame and glory, and to suicide, pain, and suffering, and all of that, but you have to stop absolutely still and flow with the stream. In that flowing, which involves living in each moment, a true faith is born that the stream of life will not take you anywhere that is bad.

G: There is no fear involved. In a quiet moment, or in a quiet space, there is tremendous energy and there is a tremendous capacity to see everything differently, to see it anew and afresh. If you look at whatever you encounter with that quietness, you live an entirely different kind of life than if you examine things from the perspective of thought.

A: It is such a relief to realize that you don't have to do anything except to be aware of the present moment. And you will know, instinctively, exactly what the right action is in that moment; whether it is to get a better job, so that you can support your family in the way that they have to be supported, or whether it is only necessary to remain quiet and give complete attention to 'what is.'

G: No matter what action it brings in your daily life.

A: You will be guided, inwardly, by the stream of life, and you don't have to do a thing except to fulfill — moment by moment, as completely as you can — what life requires you to do. For example, look at the things that you and I have done; they've all imperceptibly led us to the place where we now are. The things that we did were not motivated by personal achievement, personal gain, ambition, or anything like that, at least on my part; I can't speak for you. I was only interested in finishing off each particular thing so that my mind would no longer be trapped by it; so that I wouldn't wake up in the middle of the night wondering how it would be to live in the tropics, or how it would be to live in Latin America.

G: You were living it through and completing it.

A: And it has dropped away. Now I feel free of it. I don't have to go to the tropics anymore, even though I love the tropics; I don't have to go there anymore. I don't have to own an airplane anymore. I don't have to own an Arabian horse anymore. So those things have dropped away, because I didn't condemn my interest in them; I let the situation flower. I was interested, so after giving them my full attention, they naturally withered away.

G: I was trying to expand on the state of having a quiet mind, which is very hard. And that's why I said that it is more then just a split second in time between two thoughts.

A: I don't know. That is something that each person would have to experience for himself.

G: Well, I think it contains other elements.

A: Isn't the present moment what we're talking about? A total perception, observation, and non-directional attention to the present moment is what is involved in having a quiet mind. In a way, it is only the thought process that is quiet, because it has not identified itself with any of the bits of the present moment. That's the reason the thinking process is quiet. Actually, of course, a thousand things are happening in the present moment; it isn't really a state of quietness from that point of view. The dog may be scratching, the cat may be meowing, and so on.

G: It is a state of total awareness, in which there is everything.

A: Right.

G: A state in which there are many possibilities; we can go into any of them, or we can just stay with the moment.

A: The quietness is not present in the things that are being perceived; the quietness exists because the mind has not identified with any fragment of the holistic experience and run off with it. There is no stillness of the mind in that, and so other things are not perceived. But if there is a quietness in the mind, there is a total perception of everything around you, which might even include a thunder and lightning storm. But you, as a thinking individual, are quiet because you've seen how limiting it is to identify with any segment of the totality of the moment. Wonderful things may be happening around you that can very definitely influence your life and affect your well-being. But if you are not paying attention, you're not aware of whatever might be trying to tell you something very, very important at that moment. Do you see what I mean?

G: Yes.

A: So if you see all of that, at least see the possibility of it intellectually, then there is a real incentive for having a quiet mind. That could be an incentive for undertaking the tremendous job of disposing of all of the unfinished business that you've accumulated.

G: I would use the word interest, rather than motive or incentive, because that's what it is.

A: All right, so that will provide the interest. In other words, if you're suffering and you've got a stomachache, there is an interest in not suffering and having a stomachache. You're interested in what is causing it and what you can do to alleviate it. In the same way, when you realize how you have cut yourself off from all of the wonderful things that are happening around you each and every moment, it generates the interest required to observe the situation. And whenver you catch yourself identifying with a fragment and running off with it, you drop it. You pick up the ball through force of habit and you run with it for a couple of steps; then you suddenly become aware of what you have done, and you drop the ball. You don't have to throw it away, you don't have to push it away, you don't have to say, "I mustn't think about it." Perception is there, and intelligence brings about the right action.

G: Do you do anything consciously to continue that state?

A: Any thought you have about it is part of the old habit pattern.

G: And you drop it again.

A: Every time; it is a constant rejection of the thinking process, except where it is needed. No effort or will is involved in this rejection.

EXPLORING THE
WORLDS BEYOND THOUGHT

*In the light of awareness thought
ceases, and life creates a
state of pure insight.*

G: Just what do you mean by "exploring the worlds beyond thought," which is, of course, the subtitle of your book, NOW-CONSCIOUSNESS?

A: You know, I always thought that was an intriguing title, because it wasn't meant to be just a catchy phrase, or a catchy title. It really has some meaning behind it, and I'd like to go into what I intended by it, because it concerns the whole quest for now-consciousness. First, consider the word 'exploring;' under what conditions can we explore anything? In order to explore something, you have to start from where you happen to be at a particular moment, don't you? You can explore intellectually; for instance, you can explore Russia or some other part of the world in your mind, but it would only be in your mind, wouldn't it?

G: You'd be using past knowledge to explore.

A: That's right; in other words, you'd be using the thought process to explore. But to explore the worlds beyond thought would be to explore without the thinking process. How can we explore the worlds without the thinking process, unless we start in the now? Because the present moment, as we've said before, requires no thought, only attention. You and I are both sitting here, and we are surrounded by all of the tangible things that are in this room, as well as the other intangible things that are probably here, such as radio and television signals, etc., that we can't see or taste or smell or sense without the proper equipment. All of these would have to comprise the point from which exploration would have to begin; they have nothing to do with thought. The things in this room, although they were thought-created originally by somebody, are not a part of thought at this present moment. They only become a part of thought when you happen to concentrate or focus your attention upon specific items. Otherwise they are beyond thought. This present moment is beyond thought.

In other words, what I'm trying to say is that the perception of something beyond thought doesn't require a mysterious, occult, or especially high state of consciousness. It is not some exotic state that can only be experienced after living a certain kind of lifestyle. Everybody is in contact with the present moment, every day of their life. So exploration into what is beyond thought would be an exploration into the true values of life as they actually exist at any given moment, because the world of thought is obviously the world that society has created. It is our complex social structure, it is the business world, it is our home life, it is our relationship with other people — how we approach all of the relationships that we are involved in — all comprise a part of the thought structure. This is the world of thought.

The whole idea of now-consciousness is to give complete

attention to and completely perceive the present that exists at any given moment. So exploration of that means that you have to start with where you are, 'what is,' at any moment. Anyone can do it. It isn't something unique, or something special. Anyone can do it, that's the whole point.

So we've determined that exploration has to begin here and now. It is always the next step, provided it is an exploration into the facts of life, not our ideas about them. We're not exploring the worlds of thought; that world has been explored by everyone who has lived on this planet. The records of those explorations can be found in all the existing literature and in the knowledge passed down to us through tradition.

G: But how do you leave thought behind?

A: Well, that's kind of jumping the gun. I think the first question would be: What is thought, and what triggers thought? In other words, if we are not completely enmeshed in thought, what is it that triggers the thinking process? What is it that triggers our jumping on the so-called 'thought-train' and taking a ride?

G: Knowledge, that which I already know.

A: Would you say that knowledge is another term for memory, that memory is a part of knowledge?

G: Yes.

A: So memory triggers the thought process. Suppose life presents me with a particular situation, a certain challenge. If aspects of the challenge correspond to a memory within my field of consciousness, then that memory is elicited by the challenge. The process resembles retrieving a photograph from a photographic album, or obtaining a readout from a computer. The memory itself elicits a train of thought from our consciousness which is linked to that particular memory. The memory is like a computer button; we push the computer button and out comes a readout. The particular train of thought associated with a memory is analogous to a computer readout. We then take a ride on that particular 'thought-train' until life presents us with another challenge (which brings that thought to an end), or the thought, because of similarities, continues on in a different form; it is through associated memories that one thought leads into another, and another. Most of the time we are caught in an endless chain of thinking. It seems to be that that is the origin of what we call thinking.

G: If memory is the origin of thinking, what produces the memory?

A: Obviously, there seem to be several kinds of memory, aren't there? But the memory that seems to prevent us from meeting the present factually is what we call psychological memory. We need to question the origin of psychological memory. Do you have any ideas about it?

G: Well, I think feelings are very much involved in it — it has emotional content.

A: Yes, that's true; feelings are involved. But we have all had the experience of acting spontaneously, according to insight, or according to some challenge that came up that demanded a creative response. Such a response seems to bypass our personal memory, taking us beyond our personal ego-drive.

G: As in a crisis, where there is instant action.

A: Yes, as in acts of sudden bravery or heroism, or in other actions in which people are taken completely out of themselves and act spontaneously. And when the event is over, is there any psychological memory connected with it? There's memory connected with it, but the memory is of the editing that we did after the event happened, of the thinking that we did, in which we introduced the idea of ourselves.

We try to remember what we did and how we did it. We begin to supply reasons and excuses, and provide explanations for the act of heroism or bravery. We identify ourselves with it, and remember that we were the ones that were brave; we did it, when somebody else did not. Isn't that where psychological memory enters the picture, in that type of action? But it is not a memory of the action itself, because the action was so spontaneous, so correct, so true, and so direct, that no memory was connected with it.

G: I see the difference, yes.

A: On the personal level, at least, there was no memory. The only thing that we remember is what we did with it afterwards; in other words, thought was an accessory after the fact!

G: Yes.

A: So I would say that psychological memory is like a photographic album of all of those events that have happened to us during our lifetime; at times there was direct action, right action, but the memory of those acts are not in the album. The actions that we perform as egocentric individuals, in life, always have psychological memory connected with them.

G: Yes, because all of that is a part of the content of consciousness.

A: Yes; the content of consciousness (as we have said at other times) is everything that human beings have ever thought. All of our ideas, all of our values, all of our ideals, all of our strivings, loves, hatreds, joys, happiness, and pleasure — all of that is part of human consciousness.

G: Yes, and it is usually retrievable through the linkage or the tie-in with the emotional content which surrounds those events, or those facts.

A: I think the emotional content determines the extent to which a certain event is recorded in our psychological memory.

G: Yes. Why is thought fragmentary?

A: Well, I see it as fragmentary because, in watching my own thought, or in being aware of the thinking process, I see that it is impossible for me to think about more than one thing at a time. I can think about any one object in this room, or any one idea, but this is a linear progression of thought, moving from one detail to another, isn't it?

G: Yes.

A: You can't think about the totality of life. You can't think about the totality of this room — all that is in this room, you and I and everything that's happening — except in a linear way, step by step, piece by piece; and as we said before, we have learned to do it so rapidly that we believe that we are thinking about the whole thing. We've been satisfied with this, but to me it is always fragmentary.

G: What is the difference then between knowledge — working always from the known, the memory — and a state of knowing?

A: A state of knowing is obviously in the present, isn't it? In other words, we can know that we are sitting here, we know that we have our feet on the floor, we know our relationship to everything in this room. That's a knowing which is always in the present, never in the past or the future. But knowledge pertains to the world that man has created by thought, doesn't it? It is all of the memories, it is all of the remembered pieces of information, that are used in our educational system, in our halls of learning, and that are contained in all of the books in the libraries.

In other words, knowledge is equivalent to the information in our personal memory bank, the readout we get when we push a certain button with a certain name on it; it emerges in the form of knowledge, personal knowledge. And then there is human knowledge, which is contained in all of the books in the libraries and educational institutions. This is all knowledge, that which humanity has experienced in the past.

Knowledge is always two-dimensional, and that is one of the reasons why I think that it is dangerous that our social structure, our society, and the actions of the people involved, are always based upon knowledge. Their actions are always based upon how people acted before in similar situations. All of the laws, all of the rules, all of the things that we go by, are all based upon a two-dimensional outlook on life. Everything is always based on the past, on what somebody did in the past. If a law is to be interpreted by a jury, for instance, it has to be done in accordance with interpretations given in the past.

G: Precedence.

A: But knowing is a quality of the present moment; it includes a holistic feeling about life as it is and as it really exists at that moment.

G: I see. What is the origin of the idea of time?

A: Is there such a thing as time in this present moment?

G: Physical time, chronological time.

A: It is a thought, an idea.

G: It is a convenience.

A: But it is still an idea.

G: But we use it as a fact.

A: No, don't look at the clock.

G: I look at the clock and it is a quarter to nine.

A: But that's all an idea, it has nothing to do with the present moment. You are bringing it into the present moment as a thought, but it is not a part of the present moment.

G: But I'm calling physical time a convenience. If we have an appointment at nine o'clock, we have to take it into consideration.

A: But you're getting away from the present moment by bringing it in.

G: But some people would say this is the present moment; it is a quarter to nine, and if I have an appointment at nine o'clock I have to prepare.

A: You see how easy it is to get away from the present moment? It really is, you know. Through your action just now, you answered your own question: "What is the origin of time?" The origin of time was in your mind when you looked at the clock and said what you did. So isn't that always the origin of time? Obviously chronological time exists. We can look at the clock and we know that after a certain number of minutes it is going to be another time. But I am talking about psychological time, the idea of time which always puts so much pressure on us. Isn't it involved in our ideas about performance and competition, and in many of the stress-related problems found in our present society?

In the natural world I don't see such a thing as time. I see time only in relationship to our ideas about it. If you don't use memory to look back, or if you don't use your imagination to look ahead, is there such a thing as time?

G: No, then there's only the moment.

A: You have to use thought to look backward, don't you?

G: Yes.

A: But you can't use thought in the present moment. Thought has no significance in the present moment. It only has significance when you want to tie the present moment to something in the past through memory, or dream up some future which you hope to achieve. Isn't thought always the first step out of the present moment? If that is true, then thought would have to be the origin of time; time couldn't take place without thought.

G: That's right, because thought always brings in the past; it is the link from the past to what we try to form in the future.

A: Thought is always going into the past, or it is going into the future; but the present moment doesn't need to be thought about. For instance, wouldn't it seem ridiculous if I was sitting here telling you, "I want you to think about your hand, I want you to think about sitting on that chair, I want you to think about all the things that you are experiencing at this present moment?" You would think that was ridiculous, because it is obvious that we don't have to think about these things. There's a 'knowing' quality about our relationship to things, isn't there?

Really, I see the whole thing as very, very simple; it is so simple that most people seem to have trouble grasping it. They are looking for a complicated answer, because the world of thought has become so complicated (in terms of the values, and names, and ideas that people have added to it over the ages) that they think the answer has to be complex. But from my point of view, it is so simple that everybody misses it. The simplicity lies in what is happening right at this moment; there is a knowing in you and I right now as to exactly what our relationship is to everything around us.

G: If thought has put all of this together, how can one go beyond it?

A: Can thought go beyond?

G: How can it? And what could go beyond? How can one go beyond?

A: A new factor must obviously be introduced in order to transcend the thought process; and once again, we should be able to go into it right from this present moment. Does anything exist in this present moment that is not a part of thought, and that is not a part of our personal memory bank and ego?

G: I would say awareness, perception, and the factual things we are surrounded by.

A: I think that you're right. I feel that perception is something that is beyond thought, because perception is inherent in every living creature in the world. Every living creature has perception, and is able to use perception within its own particular field of consciousness.

G: Yes.

A: I think the problem that exists is that we have identified ourselves with perception. We say that *we're* perceiving, or *we're* feeling, or *we're* smelling, or *we're* doing. I think that these are all ideas, because from a factual point of view there is only seeing, there is only doing, there is only feeling, there is only smelling, there is only hearing; it is only an idea that *we* are seeing, *we* are hearing, *we* are smelling, *we* are feeling these things. I believe that each person has to explore this themselves, and see if it is true; does perception exist beyond our personal ideas about it?

To me, it is a very real fact that perception is outside my field of consciousness. It is completely separate from the thought process. When my mind is quiet, there is complete perception; there is no fragmentation due to my personal identification with one object.

G: But the moment that I say that I am aware of that beautiful sunset, I bring in my ego, or I bring in the 'I' of thought. I create a memory, so that tomorrow I can say, "Yesterday I saw a beautiful sunset."

A: That's right; in other words, we take a mental picture of something the minute we identify with it and say, "I have seen it," or "I am seeing it." I must remember it, because it is a beautiful picture and I want to put it into my photographic album so that tomorrow I can drag it out and compare it with something else that I've seen, or so that I can tell you about it."

G: That's how we generate our own personal body of knowledge.

A: It is also a matter of communication. We can't communicate with another person without using words or ideas. Communication on the physical level has to be through the field of consciousness, doesn't it?

G: Yes.

A: I can communicate to you things that I have experienced, or things that I'm experiencing at the present time. I can do it through words, or I can do it through memory, but I have to use the field of human consciousness. I have to use the values, the words, and everything else that we both understand in order to get the idea across to you.

But your perception of an idea doesn't have to involve the field of consciousness. A sudden understanding or a sudden knowing may occur inside of you when you hear me talking about something or describing it. And even though I'm using my conditioning to describe it, you don't have to use your conditioning to understand it. That's the point.

G: I can use now-consciousness to understand it.

A: Right! This is very important, because it creates an entirely new situation. In other words, you or I or anyone else who is endeavoring to communicate a certain idea or a certain insight has to use accepted grammatical forms in order to be understood. But the holistic understanding of the other person has to lie outside of the field of human consciousness. If the person who is listening is understanding or interpreting the words in a mechanical way only, then that person's understanding is only on the verbal level; it doesn't go any deeper, and it doesn't affect the person's actions. For your actions in life to be really affected at the gut level, you have to understand things outside of the field of your personal conditioning. You can't be caught by any of the words that you hear. You can't bring up something out of your memory bank, or bring up some photograph that you've personally taken, some memory, and have understanding take place. The minute you catch yourself interpreting something in any way at all — going back to your memory bank in any way at all — drop it. In dropping the memory, you are open again and free of your conditioning. Once free, understanding can take place at a deep level, and this can really change your life.

This is why Krishnaji had such difficulty in communicating with the people who listened to him; most of them were interpreting the words that he was using. They were mired down by the ideas that were evoked in their minds by the words that he used, and they made no impression on them at a deep level. Consequently, there was no understanding. They would say, "I understand what Krishnamurti is talking about, it is very plain what he's talking about," but there was no inner revolution in their understanding of life.

G: So it became another accumulation of ideas.

A: Exactly, there was no inner revolution. The inner revolution can only take place outside the field of consciousness. There has to be *a* listening, not *you* listening; there has to be a listening without 'you' in the picture. And when there is that listening, then what is heard is not being interpreted, it is not being analyzed, and it is not being filtered through your conditioning. In that, there's a holistic understanding which affects you at a deep level, and changes your life, and brings about this inner revolution that Krishnaji was talking about.

G: That's right.

A: I think that is the whole secret of it.

G: Yes. So this perception, this awareness is necessary. If one is in a state of now-consciousness, then what is beyond that? What is beyond man's creation, beyond man's whole field of the known? What happens? Let us go into that now.

A: Well, the world of nature is beyond; understanding, love, affection, attention, compassion, beauty, and all of the so-called virtues are beyond; everything that humanity has ever dreamed about possessing, but has never really possessed except as a name or idea, is beyond human consciousness. And it is not something that can't be touched at any time, because what is beyond human consciousness (as we said before) is the present moment. Thus beauty can be touched in the present moment if I'm not in the picture, "I" as an idea. Affection can be touched in the present moment; love can be touched in the present moment; understanding can be touched. All of the things that we have just named can be touched in the present moment.

G: Yes.

A: It is so simple everybody passes it by, because most of us expect a complicated answer. You have to experiment and really discover for yourself the simple beauty of this approach to life.

G: It is so direct.

A: Absolutely direct; direct perception, direct action.

G: So how does one wake up? How does one stay in the now?

A: Well, let us start in this present moment again, because this is the beginning point. Every step, every question has to begin with this present moment. Would you ask the question, "How can I sit in this chair?"

G: No, I guess I know how.

A: "How can I put my feet on the floor? How can I put my two hands together? How can I look at another person?" You know, it is so simple. There's no how to it for us. So the question is not how to do something in a positive way, but rather what prevents us from doing it? That should be the question. What prevents me from being aware that I'm sitting in this chair? What prevents me from being aware that I have my hands clasped together and my thumbs are moving together against each other? What prevents me from being aware of this?

G: All that we've been talking about.

A: Right; thought.

G: Thought.

A: In other words, identification with a certain object or a certain idea that was recalled through the memory process, a retrieval from our personal memory bank. That's what prevents us from being constantly attentive and aware of what is happening in the present moment.

G: Then without awareness there is no true love, no beauty, no compassion, no affection, none of those things that are beyond thought.

A: They don't exist, if I'm thinking.

G: No.

A: They can't. Each one can exist as an idea; I can name each one as an abstraction. But it is just an idea, it is not the thing itself. The emotions themselves, which are part of the holistic feeling about life which contains all of those so-called virtues, are there every moment. But we're simply not aware of them because we're busy thinking about some picayune idea that has nothing to do with them at all.

Of course, you have to use thought in order to make plans. If you have a certain insight into what has to be done this afternoon, or tomorrow, or whatever, you have to use thought. You have to use the creative planning capacity of your brain in order to bring it about. But most of the time we're not in that situation; most of the time we could sit back and enjoy these other things that we've been talking about as possibilities. We could enjoy them as facts, and not just as ideas.

G: In other words, I don't see nature when I'm thinking.

A: Of course not.

G: I can see that that's a tree, or a bird, and so on, but I don't really see it, feel it, or perceive it when the mind is chattering.

A: The minute you name something you don't perceive it, either. You perceive the tree, and the minute you name the tree, the perception is gone. In the act of naming, the name you are giving the tree becomes superimposed between you and the tree. The same phenomenon takes place in every phase of our life.

G: Seeing the beauty of what we're saying, and the necessity of it, and perhaps experiencing it — how does it come about?

A: I think we should start once again with something that we can understand. Obviously, thought cannot wake itself up. I consider thinking a form of dreaming. (People call it thinking,

109

you know, but actually it is day-dreaming!) Thought can't wake itself up. If you're in the middle of a dream at night, you normally can't wake yourself up immediately. However, there are certain techniques that the occultists use to trick themselves into waking up in the middle of a dream; they then go on with the dream in a different way, objectively.

G: They're experimenting with this now in dream labs.

A: There's the possibility of doing this. There's also the possibility of waking yourself up and becoming aware of the fact that you have been thinking a certain train of thought. Then, instead of continuing that particular thought (which, from your point of view, might be a negative thought), you continue in the thought process by substituting what you consider to be a more positive, more acceptable thought.

G: That's still the same old thing. It is still using memory to trick yourself into thinking in another way.

A: So both ways are really tricks of the mind, aren't they?

G: Yes.

A: So, if thought cannot wake itself up, if thought cannot bring itself to an end, if thought cannot extricate itself from the field of human consciousness — which is the origin of thought in the first place — then something else has to take place, doesn't it? Another factor must come into play to break the impasse. Earlier, we came to the realization that perception and awareness are outside of human consciousness. So what is it that will wake us up? That was the question you asked.

G: Just now you said thought can't achieve its own end. What do you mean by that? You can't think yourself to the end of thought?

A: No, there has to be some outside agency, doesn't there? There has to be some factor outside of my conditioned response.

G: You said that thought can't stop itself. You can't sit there and say, "I'm going to meditate and stop thinking?"

A: No, because consciously stopping a negative type of thought, for instance, and turning it into a positive thought, is still continuing the thought process. Some of the so-called New-Thought organizations do this type of mental manipulation; they tell you to think positively instead of negatively. It is just a trick of the mind. In other words, they continue to experience the same dream, only they've edited it now, and they turn it into a positive dream instead of a negative one.

But this doesn't answer your question, and I think it is an intriguing question. I like to use analogies, because I think analogies are really another way of talking about harmonics on another level. For example, you yourself have thoroughly studied and used your mind and your mental capacity to its utmost to determine all of the facts concerning a certain way of living. You've gone as far as you can go in creatively thinking about the subject, and have used your mental capacity to find out everything related to the healing work that you do. Is that true?

G: Yes, it is.

A: Then suppose that somebody calls you this afternoon and tells you that your assistance is required tomorrow morning at 8:00, that the capacity that you've developed as a 'healer' is needed to help someone. You realize the value of doing this, you see that life has chosen you to do this and that you have the capacity to do it, and you have a feeling that you can perhaps help this other person. Are you going to need an alarm clock to wake you in time to be ready for your 8 o'clock appointment tomorrow morning? Or are you going to wake up spontaneously?

G: I'll wake up by myself.

A: You'll wake up. You won't need an alarm clock. You may set one just as a safety measure because you may not be completely sure you'll wake up, but you will always awaken. Just as I'd wake up if somebody called me and wanted to talk about my favorite subject, now-consciousness. I would wake up; I wouldn't need an alarm clock because I'm intensely interested in the subject, just as you are intensely interested in what you are doing, too. We can't say it is 'you' waking yourself up, or 'me' waking myself up. It is the interest that we have in the things with which we are involved that wakes us up. That interest is part of the life-force, the vitality or energy of life, that awakens us. Isn't that true?

G: Yes, one can hardly wait to get started.

A: Well, if this is true on the physical level, why doesn't it apply on other levels as well? Wouldn't it apply to waking up from a thought pattern?

G: It is part of that inner intention, that interest.

A: Suppose that I have gone into this deeply enough to see the value and the logic of waking up. I realize that most of the time I identify with just one fragment of each moment. I can see the potential danger in this limited response to unforeseen challenges and am really serious in my desire to change. I see that I will be unable to cope adequately with emergencies that may come up as long as I'm plugged into only one channel. Suppose that you have told me all of this, and I've looked into it and understood logically at least that what you say must be true. I may not have felt it deeply because I have not experienced it myself, but I see that life must be much richer; there must be a thousand things out there of which I'm unaware.

My inquiry and deep interest opens the door for insight. There is freedom from the known, because I clearly see that thought cannot make a breakthrough. Another factor, outside of myself, must become operative. In other words, I can't consciously awaken myself from sleep, nor can I consciously bring about awareness.

Perceiving the validity of these observations gives me the inner intention to wake up, and this inner incentive accomplishes what thought cannot do. Thought can't extricate itself from the trap it has created. It is the sincere acknowledgement of this impasse that opens the door for insight to occur.

G: That's exactly it.

A: If I've reached that stage mentally, and have really pushed it and am really interested, my inquiry and my interest are going to be the very things that wake me up.

G: And then you carry that through into action. When someone comes to you with a problem, you approach it with an attitude of 'I' don't know. For example, I can't approach the healing process with any knowledge that I have; but if I stay away from thought and just 'tune' into the energy that is there, that exists in that same state of perception, the healing may occur.

A: Exactly.

G: And if you take that approach when someone comes to you with a question, rather than approaching it from the standpoint of what you've already written or thought or experienced, then real communication may occur. Or you may at least say something important to that person; whether they can apprehend it in the same way or not is not your responsibility.

A: You are not personally providing the answer. If you are open, if your cup is empty, and life is pouring information into you moment by moment through the medium of insight, then you are not consciously saying something designed to engender a particular reaction in the other person. If you have the idea that you are going to effect a certain result, it is a product of thought.

G: That's right. 'I' am not a healer, 'I' can't heal anybody.

A: You will spontaneously and intuitively say the right thing, with no idea at all as to why you are saying it. And it is life that engenders the understanding in the other person that might change the course of that person's life. But you are not doing it to bring about a specific result; that is the important point.

People thought that Krishnaji deliberately said certain

things to them personally that were designed to elicit particular results, because specific results did occur as a consequence of what he said. But I don't believe that he himself had any intention of doing that; he said what he did because at that moment it was the right thing to say. It was life that engendered an understanding in the listener.

G: Yes, because that energy, that life, that love that comes through, is then actually working in that state beyond thought. And that is the state of pure insight and pure compassion, and in that state, healing and understanding can take place.

What do you think Krishnaji meant by saying that you must follow a thought to its end?

A: If I've suddenly awakened to the fact that my mind has been identifying with a certain train of thought, there are two directions in which I can go, aren't there? Usually that direction is forward; I use thought and imagination to conclude the particular thought that I had been involved in at the time I awakened. In other words, I analyze my thought, interpret the thought that I've just had, and follow it through to a conclusion of some kind. That would involve the thinking process, wouldn't it?

G: Yes.

A: In other words, it would be impossible to proceed from the point at which you have awakened without using thought.

G: So Krishnaji couldn't have meant that, could he?

A: No.

Let's go back to the analogy of sleeping. When you wake

up in the morning, there's an immediate awareness of the fact that you are in the bed where you went to sleep (if everything is normal). An awareness of how you went to sleep at night, of how you prepared yourself for bed, of all of the events leading up to it — all of this comes to you in a flash when you wake up in the morning. You don't have to think about it; in a flash you see the whole backward track. You even picture some of the dreams that your mind was involved in during the night.

In the same way, at a different and higher harmonic level, you can wake up or suddenly become aware of the fact that you've been involved in thought. Immediately, instead of proceeding, instead of analyzing and editing the thought, and all of the rest of that process, be aware of your tendency to do this, and the minute that you start doing it, drop it. In that dropping there is a clear seeing of the whole backward path. You see the train of thought that you were involved with and how it originated. You see the memory that triggered it; you see the life challenge that triggered it — you see the name, or the person, or whatever it was that triggered that particular train of thought. You can then perceive where the thought originated, how it started in your mind, how you were conditioned to react to a particular thing, and how you programmed yourself to respond in a particular way. And then the thought can even be traced back into all kinds of other little channels, back to the actual origin of the memory itself. When all of that is clearly seen, it dissipates, it withers away. It is no more, and you will not be troubled by that particular memory again.

G: Are you saying that it diminishes, that the content goes out of it, as well as the feelings associated with it?

A: The feelings go out of it, the life goes out of it, and it shrivels up in the light of understanding. It withers away in the light of awareness that you focus upon the backward path leading up to the whole train of thought. But if you make the mistake of going forward, you give it new energy, you give it new life, you give it new continuity; and then it keeps coming up over and over again, and there's no end to it. It becomes a neurotic response.

G: And there is no end to it at all.

A: So that's what I feel that Krishnaji meant when he spoke of following thought to an end; he knew that if you followed it forward it would lead to a dead end, that you'd never escape it, and that you would discover for yourself that you could never escape it.

G: Is following thought to an end different then from analysis?

A: Oh yes, completely; analysis is going forward with thought. Analysis is going forward, but also looking back while you're going ahead and analyzing the thing that you thought you were thinking about. Analysis is part of the thought process.

Now-Consciousness is the world beyond thought, where there is love, compassion, beauty, and a holistic unity with all of life.

ENLIGHTENMENT

*When the self-center ceases, there is an
entirely different energy that creates
insight, which brings enlightenment
and the perfume of compassion.*

G: The word enlightenment is used so casually these days.
Just what does enlightenment mean to you?

A: Well, the word enlightenment suggests a static state, a
state in which there is no movement. I would rather use the
word enlighten, because it is a verb, and according to the
dictionary it means to illuminate, to furnish knowledge, to
instruct, or to give spiritual insight into whatever question
happens to arise at a particular moment. I think that I would
rather discuss the topic from that perspective.

However, there apparently is a state in which a person
does experience a spiritual transformation, because it is spoken
of in many contexts. For instance, the Buddhist religion speaks
of self-realization as a turning-about at the deepest seat of
consciousness. The Christian religion speaks of regeneration,
or the rebirth of Christ, or the rebirth of intelligence deep
within the individual. Some of the psychologists, such as Jung

and Maslow, talk of individuation, and Krishnamurti talks about an inner revolution. People in many different societies around the world have experienced similar states, because such experiences apparently have been described since the existence of historical records.

I think that it is important to explore the subject of enlightenment. I'm glad that you asked the question, because there are so many different religious sects, organizations, and *gurus* in the world today who are sending out literature about enlightenment and saying, "Just listen to us and you'll be enlightened."

According to a survey taken by the Los Angeles Times a few years ago, at least 30% of those polled had experienced some religious change in their life, or had reached a point at which they suddenly perceived a certain truth; 20% said that they had experienced a deep, fundamental change in their lifestyle as a result of what they had suddenly discovered about their religion, or their philosophy. In my own case, I became a Theosophist about 1933, and my values changed and my ideas about life changed. My interests changed radically, and for the next ten years I was sold on that particular system of belief. But I think that the word enlightenment is used too commonly nowadays.

G: Like the word love.

A: It doesn't have the life or the significance anymore that it used to have. We get letters in the mail saying, "If you just take our particular course, or do the particular thing we talk about, you'll reach enlightenment." That implies, of course, that the people who are promulgating that particular idea are enlightened themselves! I wonder about that; I wonder how many people in this world are really enlightened.

I think we should explore the question of what is really meant by enlightenment. Of course, any speculation that we do about enlightenment, unless we have experienced something radical ourselves, is only speculation. Any second-hand information obtained from books or tradition must be questioned. As Jesus is purported to have said, "By their acts ye shall know them."

Can we separate ideas about enlightenment from enlightenment itself? From my point of view, there's a vast difference between an idea about something and the thing itself. If there is such a thing as actual enlightenment, what kinds of changes does it bring about in a person's life? Is it something that is achieved by oneself? Is it something that is the result of one's own efforts, or is it something that comes from the outside?

G: Let's first look at what might possibly create the opportunity for enlightenment to occur. What could bring it about? Let's talk about real enlightenment, not just the little bit of insight that seems to be meant these days, as in the seminars that are offered that say that you'll see something about yourself and therefore you'll be enlightened.

A: I think that perhaps we should start from where we happen to be right at this present moment. To be enlightened about something, according to the dictionary, means to shed light upon a particular subject. Thus there can be a state of enlightenment, or there can be an actual moment of enlightenment, on any particular topic. If we want to be enlightened about something, what is the first step?

G: To investigate it.

A: You have to investigate it; it takes inquiry. Therefore, I would say that the prerequisite to any enlightenment — whether it is a little enlightenment, a single flash of inspiration, a deep insight, or something that fundamentally changes us — must be deep inquiry. If I'm investigating some scientific problem that I'm working on, I have to go into it as deeply as possible. This is apparently what happened to Einstein, as well as to some other people who have worked on scientific projects. They pushed and pushed, and used their intellect to discover everything that was known about a particular subject, and enlightenment suddenly occurred.

Thus, you might say that, in some ways, enlightenment is synonymous with insight. You have a certain insight into a situation, and apparently that insight comes from outside of yourself, doesn't it? It doesn't come from the intellect; it is not a product of thought. Intellect prepares the ground; it clears away all of the known by investigating the subject and discovering that known information does not lead to answers. That clears the field and opens the door — empties the cup, so to speak — for insight or enlightenment to occur concerning that particular subject.

G: Yes, it's quite often been said that solutions to mathematical and scientific problems come only when the person involved has given it a rest, and has either slept on it, gone for a walk or reached a state in which they can no longer think or speculate about the problem. When the mind lets go, when the brain lets go, then the answer seems to come, from what you're referring to as the outside. But let's go deeper; let's not talk just about a little fragmentary insight, which may be a part of the foundation for total enlightenment. Do you think that there is such a thing as total enlightenment? In other words, is there an end to enlightenment?

A: I don't see enlightenment as a static state; and if it isn't a static state, there's obviously no end to it. There is enlightenment upon enlightenment upon enlightenment. This is obviously the way it's worked in our everyday life. You and I have been enlightened about many different things during our lifetimes. I don't think that there is any end to it, because the world seems to me to be such an absolutely incredible combination of things and events that I can't see there ever being an end to it. You might be enlightened about everything that exists on this particular planet, but think about how many planets there are in the universe.

Earlier we discussed what was necessary to bring about insight, and decided that it was pushing the known to its limits; when we get to the limits of the known, then something else can happen. Therefore, I would say that the necessary prerequisite for enlightenment is freedom from the known.

What is the known? The known is everything that we have learned; all of our ideas, all of our philosophies, all of our religious ideas, and all of our traditional concepts about life. That's what the known is; and it is not just my known, it is the known of all humanity. It is the sum total of what we call human consciousness. We don't know what the limits of that consciousness are, but consciousness as we know it is where we human beings function. Consciousness, which has been developed by individual reactions to life over countless generations, has developed into what we call human consciousness, and that is the known.

Therefore, if there is a state of enlightenment, or a plateau which we can reach, or which can occur in our lifetime, it would have to be a condition in which there was freedom from the known. We'd have to be free of the known. Not that we wouldn't use the known, because you have to use the known to communicate; you have to use the known to write books; you have to use the known to relate to others.

G: You have to use the known to function.

A: You have to use it to function; you have to use it as a tool, but be free of it so that there is a possibility of exploring what is beyond.

G: You mean that you have to be free of the psychological content, the emotional content.

A: Yes; not free of factual things, but free of our ideas about them and our psychological ties to them.

G: In other words, the 'I' cannot be enlightened; in fact, it is ridiculous to think in that way, of the 'I' reaching enlightenment. As long as I'm working from the known, motivated by my ego, by my desire, by what I would love to achieve (no matter how grand and glorious the goal might be), I can't possibly reach it.

A: No, because if your goal is freedom from the known, you can't achieve it by going from the known to the unknown. You can explore the known and everything within the realm of the known; you can go to every corner of the earth and explore what humanity has discovered, but you can't take this additional step. In other words, we have not created the boat by which we can cross the river. The river can be crossed, but we cannot cross it by our own efforts, or by means of any boat or other form of transportation that we've made with thought.

G: Then how does one approach the problem? I see an underlying fundamental drive — perhaps a passion, in the true sense of the word — in people. Many of us seem to have this longing for clarity, an inner drive towards being one with life, as I would phrase it. How then does one approach it? Because I think enlightenment is the basic purpose of life.

A: Yes, there seems to be an evolutionary thrust to life. As I see it, life is continually searching for ways to express itself. It expresses itself through all of the life forms that exist on the planet. I feel that the only thing that can interfere with the thrust of the life-force, or the evolution of life forms, is the development of what we call the ego, the development of the personal self-centered activities of our individual thought processes. I see that as the only thing that stands in the way.

G: Yes, that is going in just the opposite direction, isn't it?

A: It certainly is, because most people are trying desperately to maintain their egocentric way of life. We are constantly told to assert ourselves, develop our egos, develop our personalities, stand up for our rights, fight for our rights. All of these things are manifestations of the ego drive, aren't they?

G: Yes; people even say that to meditate on the self, one should study whatever people have said on the subject. In other words, gather together everything that is known about it, whether it is true or false. A lot of nonsense has been written about it, too. That whole effort of accumulating ideas in order to become a meditator is not going to bring enlightenment. I think it takes you further away from it.

125

A: That's correct, it does distance you from life. For instance, if you look at the beautiful trees, plants, flowers, animals, and all of the other beautiful things of nature, you see no ego drive in any of them. You can be sure that the tree out there isn't trying to compete with the tree next to it. It grows naturally towards the sunlight in any way that it can, and if there's a whole grove of trees, the one that has the best root system, the one that has the most nourishment in the soil, the one that gets the most moisture, the one that has the best opportunity, will grow to be the tallest and eventually get the most sunlight. Aren't we the same? We are led to believe that without the ego drive we would be nothing. We don't realize that the whole evolutionary thrust of the life-force is operating within us, just as it is in every other manifestation of life, and it will take us inevitably to our true destination, wherever that might be.

G: Yes, that's what I meant before: the underlying interest, even though it is misnamed, misused, and misguided.

A: You know, we see it in ourselves; I certainly see it in myself. I can see that at different points in my life I was very curious about certain things, and my curiosity led to enlightenment concerning those particular subjects. I think that the basic drive toward inquiry — the basic drive which makes us want to explore — is a part of life, a part of nature. You see it in everything. You see it in animals, for example; baby animals are out exploring the world and finding out what life is all about. I think that curiosity is a natural, normal thing, and without it we would obviously all remain in a static condition, and very little would happen.

G: "Seek and ye shall find."

A: Right. You know the old saying, "Curiosity killed the cat." Well, I would express it differently. I would paraphrase it, and say that curiosity killed the ego! Because the curiosity that develops the ego — which drives us on and on, to add more and more in our search for what we consider pleasure, safety, and security — eventually winds up being the thing that actually causes our demise. It kills us. It is the end of the ego. It may not be the end right at that particular moment, but it is the beginning of the end.

When you discover what makes the ego tick — this clock that you've been winding for centuries, that humanity has been winding for centuries — it is the first step towards freedom. In the beginning we are interested in the ticking; we think the ticking is great, and we give ourselves to it and keep winding the clock so that it ticks faster and faster. However, we finally get to a place where the ticking drives us mad. It drives you crazy, because you see that the ticking is preventing you from understanding the life around you. And then you suddenly discover that you're the one that is winding the clock! God isn't winding the clock; Jesus Christ isn't winding the clock; Buddha isn't winding the clock. Nobody is winding the clock but you. When you discover that you're the one that is winding the clock, causing the ticking, causing all of the problems and the conflicts, then every time you catch yourself winding it up again, you drop it, don't you? That's the end of the winding, and the clock finally runs down, because there's no more energy expended in that particular direction.

G: So one thing that one can do is to let the ego-clock run itself down.

You've talked about our innate drive to explore and understand. What else do we do, or not do, to block the state of enlightenment? It seems that so many of the things that we do close curtains instead of open windows for the Light to come in.

A: In the first place, do we really want enlightenment? Enlightenment brings about many, many changes; it induces a completely different lifestyle. I think that people have to have looked into every facet of their lives, to discover whether there is anything that they have left undone, before they even think about it.

Most people think that if they had more money they would be happy, or if they just had good health, or a different wife or husband, or different relationships, their lives would be different.

Doesn't a person have to look into all of those things until each one turns to ashes in their mouths? Ultimately, of course, they are all going to turn to ashes in our mouths, aren't they; when death comes that's the end of it. You give up every possession you've ever accumulated, and that's the end of it: period, full stop. But if you think that a certain thing will solve your problems in life and bring you happiness, you should try to obtain it. I feel that enlightenment, or regeneration, or inner revolution (or whatever you want to call it) is for very few people.

G: So you're saying that we have to live life fully.

A: In order to find out whether any particular thing has value, there has to be freedom to experiment. In other words, life to me is like a big department store, and we can get anything in it that we want to. All we have to do is pay the price; but we can have anything in this world.

128

G: But you're not talking about indulging yourself; you're talking about something else.

A: Yes, I'm talking about finding out for oneself whether any of these things bring any permanent peace. A state of enlightenment — which I don't think is a static state — has to be quite different from all of that. It can't just involve more automobiles, or more money in the bank.

G: No, of course not; we're not talking about that. We're talking about inner peace, inner quiet.

A: But people's ideas about inner peace and quietness are usually an escape from whatever is going on in their outward lives. They don't have a good relationship with their family or their friends, perhaps, and so they want peace.

G: They say to themselves, "I think I will go into a retreat; I will go into the mountains and sit quietly because my life is a shambles, and maybe I can find enlightenment and all will be solved."

A: That's right; I think that is exactly the reason most people seek enlightenment. I feel that being enlightened, in the true, deep sense that we're discussing here, is a result of an evolutionary, or developmental, movement in life. In other words, I think one has to have a certain maturity. Enlightenment can't come to you if you're still stuck at the juvenile stage of wanting more money and more cars and more love affairs; you first have to be a mature person.

If enlightenment is the culmination of something other

than one's ideas and aspiration, then the ground has to be prepared ahead of time. A person has to be morally mature. I feel that that is one of the qualities that is so lacking in most of the *gurus'* ideas about enlightenment; most of them sell enlightenment for a certain fee. But I see that quality of maturity as something that is completely missing. Nobody speaks about moral development or moral character, nobody talks about actual goodness in life or about right relationships, or any of that. They speak about enlightenment as something that is going to give them psychic powers, or something that is going to help them experience 'bouncing around between the planets,' seeing colored lights.

G: Yes, it is getting all mixed up. The psychic and the spiritual realms are seen by people as being the same thing. They seem to make no distinction anymore between religion and philsophy, or between psychic and spiritual matters.

Let's look now at the facts of enlightenment, at the changes that come about, and at how one lives differently.

A: As we said earlier, I feel that it brings about an entirely new lifestyle. It induces new values, and we see things from a different point of view.

There seem to be two different kinds of energy which we can discover for ourselves. We're all familiar with the kind of energy that is generated while we're mixed up in the ego drive. You see a certain thing, or life presents you with a certain situation, and your mind starts working on it; you dream up a picture, and imagine yourself experiencing that particular thing. This creates an energy which we call desire, and we dream up ways of accomplishing what we want to accomplish. We are all familiar with that kind of energy, but it ends when the particular desire is fulfilled. If the desire isn't fulfilled, the energy may be transferred to another object or goal. This energy is diminished if we have ill health, or if we're too tired. When old age creeps up on us, we don't have energy; and when death comes that's the end of that energy, period.

But you and I both know that there is another kind of energy. For instance, there's the energy that you yourself exhibit when you are healing people; you can work all day long. I've seen you work on 35 or 40 people in one day, and be just as full of energy at the end of the time as you were at the beginning. So you're obviously using another kind of energy, aren't you?

G: Yes, I'm not using my own energy.

A: You're not using your own energy, because if you had been, you would have been absolutely exhausted at the end of the day.

G: Yes, I would be.

A: The same thing applies to me. I can be feeling bad physically, or be tired, but if somebody comes in and wants to talk about now-consciousness or similar topics, I've got energy; I can stay up all night long and talk. I might be tired when I stop, but while I'm talking that energy is there. I think that it is the energy of life. In other words, when we are not engaged in some self-centered activity, this other energy is there to see us through, and to bring about the result that it wants to bring about.

Another thing that we have to learn is how to function without the self-center, because we're used to functioning with it constantly; until enlightenment (or this inner revolution) occurs, we're functioning from our self-center. Everything that we do comes from the self. We are always reaching out toward something that we want, or retreating inward, away from something that we don't want. And so we are constantly going back and forth, shuttling back and forth, between our self-center and the object of desire.

But when the self-center has been eliminated, or is being eliminated because we are no longer winding the clock of life, there's a different movement altogether. Then there is an outward welling all of the time. It is not just flowing from a center; the energy of life is channeling through you and accomplishing certain results in the outer world. You become a channel for life, and there's no center in a channel. If a channel had a center to it, the energy would be stopped-up halfway through. In this case, there must be an elimination of the center, so that the energy and life-force can be channeled to flow through you and accomplish things in the outer world. I think that's one definite criterion.

Another aspect that must be considered is order. The ego creates a certain order in your life; in other words, you've gotten people talked into doing things your way. You have everything arranged the way you want it — or at least as close to it as possible. I think that is typical of many people who are, either by choice or by necessity, having to live by themselves. I think it is very easy to fall into a certain pattern of behavior. But the order is very self-centered, isn't it? It is not the order of life, and that is what we're talking about: fitting into the order of life.

Still another factor that's involved in all of this is regeneration. If regeneration is a fact, which it seems to be from my point of view, where could regeneration originate? It obviously couldn't originate from an idea, because all ideas are a part of human consciousness. If I have the idea that I'm getting more and more virtuous, and that I'm fitting into the order of life, and so on, it is just an idea. To me, regeneration really takes place in the state of now-consciousness, in a state of alertness, a state of observation.

I feel regeneration actually occurs on a different level from thought. It is not the result of an idea, it is not a part of thought at all. I think this is very important to understand. Regeneration brings about an imperceptible, fundamental change at all levels of a person's being, and results in a completely new outlook on our values, our lifestyles, our ways of thinking, and our ways of using thought. Instead of using thought as a self-centered way of getting something we want and avoiding something we don't want, thought is used as a tool to create order and beauty in the environment in which we live.

G: If we are no longer moving outward from the self in order to achieve, gather, gain, or accumulate, are we still protecting that which we call the self?

A: All I can do is speak from my own experience. When this all happened to me in 1944, there was a radical transformation in my outlook on life. Since then, there has been no feeling of self-protection. One's body obviously has to be protected, because if your body isn't protected you can't function in this world at all. But there's no psychological protection, and that's the difference. Before then, there is psychological protection at all costs.

G: That's what I mean.

A: After that, after experiencing an inner revolution, there's no psychological self-protection at all, because there's nothing to protect.

G: That's right.

A: You then see that what you were protecting is what was causing all of the trouble. When you really perceive that there's no self, there can't be any self-protection.

G: So one is very open, very vulnerable.

A: Absolutely vulnerable, and I think that vulnerability is one of the characteristics of what we're talking about. Is someone who is claiming to be enlightened psychologically vulnerable, or is that person still very protective of his or her self-image?
      Another point I would like to make is that there is no psychological fear of loss. There's no fear that someone will take something from you.

G: When you lose the ego, that's the ultimate loss, isn't it? There's nothing left to lose!

A: Yes, but the ego doesn't suddenly die. Let's put it this way: it's received its death wound, but it still has to die. There's all kinds of accumulated conditioning within a person that has to be worked through. The interesting thing to me was that, from that moment in 1944 on, I was able to watch the workings of my own mind objectively, whereas before I couldn't. Before then I was involved in the process, I was identified with it, and there was no objectivity at all. I might have awakened from time to time and self-consciously realized that I had just done a certain thing, or thought a certain thing, but then there was immediate continuity in another form. But, after this inner revolution occurred, I apparently was able to use a part of my mind as a mirror, or had a new way of looking at things in an objective way.

G: The ego keeps raising its ugly head, like a many-headed monster which you slay one part at a time.

A: You become aware of that, and as soon as you wake up to the fact that this has happened, the thought drops away.

G: Living in the now always slays the dragon of thought.

A: As Krishnaji put it, the first step is the last step. You take the first step; you become aware of what you've just been involved in, and instead of taking another step into further involvement or into a continuation of the same dream, you catch yourself taking that first step and immediately the thought drops away. And when it drops away you're out in the open again, and all channels are open and available to you, not just one.

G: Yes. Is that what causes fear to stop?

A: No, I think the thing that stops fear, psychological fear, is the fact that you perceive how you have created your world of thought by all of your thinking, by all of your reactions to life. You perceive that you are the one that's created it, and that without that idea of ego, without that self-centeredness, the whole world is open to you. The perception itself brings about an end to fear in that moment. It may return if you are inattentive, but each time there is awareness, fear is gone.

G: Seeing what is, as it is.

A: Fear seems to arise in conjunction with self-protection. At the moment of awareness you see that there is nothing to protect. You see that the ego is nothing but thought. And you see that when thought is not present, the ego doesn't exist. There's no such thing as ego divorced from thought. So when thought is quiet, the mind is quiet; fear doesnt exist. But you can't think yourself out of fear. You can substitute one idea about fear for another, force yourself to think a so-called positive thought, and think you're getting rid of fear, but all you're doing is just covering it up. It will pop up when a new challenge arises. But if you catch yourself continuing the problem, that moment of awareness frees you and you're out in the open. And at that moment there is no fear. So you constantly have to be aware of the facts of your life, of what the facts are at each moment, and then there is no fear.

G: There is tremendous security in that.

A: Yes, that is the only real psychological security. There's no other security, since of course there's no ultimate physical security.

G: No, safety comes only when there's no fear.

A: Security comes when you realize that 'you' are nothing except thought. Of course, we are also a physical body and a channel for the life-force. But egotistically speaking, or psychologically speaking, we are nothing. We are an accumulation of all of the conditioning that has ever been added to our field of consciousness, and humanity's field of consciousness. And when you see what it is, it drops away; in the moment of awareness it is gone.

136

We talked earlier about enlightenment being freedom from the known. Well, part of the known consists of all of the ideas that humanity has dreamed up. One such idea is the idea of nationalism, the idea that I'm an American and some other person is a Russian, or whatever. One is an enemy and one is a friend, depending upon the economic situation; and which one is which is very important to most people.

In the state of now-consciousness none of that has any significance at all, because you realize that we're citizens of the world, we're all human beings. The planet that we're living on is the concern and responsibility of all of us. It is not just my own private little playground where I can do anything I want. We must have a feeling of responsibility toward the whole thing, because we're not here all by ourselves. The animals, the trees, the birds, the flowers, and all other things live on this planet, and we're all mutually responsible for our existence.

G: Yes, of course.

A: That suggests some other points, such as ambition. The ambition to become something was another thing that dropped away from me. People would say, "Well, without ambition what do you do, just sit around and vegetate?" No, I don't sit around and vegetate. If there is no self-centeredness to stop the flow of life, then life is using you as a channel and it is accomplishing things in the world, isn't it?

G: Exactly.

A: In other words, you become a helper to the world. You do whatever life requires of you, and you do it to the very best of your ability, providing that it coincides with the order of life. If a flower needs watering, you water it. If a tree needs care, you take care of it. If your relationship with your family needs a certain amount of love and attention, that is what you give. You know, moment by moment by moment, exactly how to fit into the order of life in a completely impersonal, unselfish way. So you really are a channel, aren't you?

G: Life seems to open up when we open up, and it brings us a tremendous new energy, as well as new ways to express that energy in our lives. Suddenly opportunities that we hadn't dreamed of ten or twenty years ago are right in front of us, and we can pursue them. We do not get involved in them for our own benefit, but for the benefit of the world we live in, and that of the people to whom we relate, and whose lives we touch.

A: This all requires honesty, doesn't it? We have to be honest in our relationships with other people. We have to be honest in ourselves. You know, the virtues that people speak of — such as honesty, and integrity, and all of those different qualities — occur on different levels. Someone might be honest because he's afraid to be dishonest, because he's afraid of the consequences.

G: That's how we're taught; don't steal, or you'll go to jail.

A: That's right; but in this new way of living, you see that honesty is part of life. You're not honest because you're afraid of being caught doing something dishonest, you're honest because it is a part of the order of life. It is a fundamental quality of life.

G: You can't be anything else.

A: No, you can't.

G: Because when you're living in the 'what is,' you can only go from that, and state that, and act from that.

A: That's right, because this flow of life, this life-force or energy, contains all of the so-called virtues, doesn't it? It contains honesty, integrity, understanding, and all of the other qualities that we have talked about.

G: When you're functioning from the ego, thought changes things for our own benefit.

A: It contaminates everything.

G: Right.

A: I feel that life has to flow through us freely, and not be stopped by the ego-center, and of course that creates a situation in which there's no conflict. There couldn't be any conflict in life then, could there? There couldn't be conflict in your relationships, or conflict between you and nature; there couldn't be conflict with anything. The free-flowing energy of life would be expressing itself through you moment by moment. You would learn to live without conflict. Most people, I think, live in a state of conflict much of the time, and in some ways conflict creates a certain energy, because being in conflict, from the ego's point of view, spurs one on. It spurs you on to avoid the conflict in some way. You change your lifestyle, or you get new associates, or you change your position in life, and so on, and that creates a certain energy and fosters the idea that you're getting somewhere.

G: Most actions seem to spring from an idea: I think I'm right, therefore I'm going to sue you; and that idea creates all kinds of conflicts, not only in my own life but in somebody else's life as well.

A: Do we really want to live without conflict? I question that in a lot of cases. I think many people don't really want to live without conflict. I don't really think some of our high government officials want to forgo conflict with the Russians, or the Nicaraguans, or others. But I'm not personally interested in conflict, and I don't see conflict in my own life. There has been an absence of conflict in my life over the past forty years, and it is wonderful to live in a state of peace.

G: Yes, now-consciousness really brings an inner peace.

A: It brings an inner peace, it brings freedom. It brings the freedom to do and say what we really feel and what we really think, because we are not afraid of conflict anymore. And the people not interested in peace don't seek our company, do they? The people that seek our company are the people that have an interest in this sort of thing, which I think involves a completely different way of living.

G: Yes; there are no games.

A: It also brings integrity, doesn't it? The word integrity, of course, is related to the word integrate, and being integrated means that all of the fragmented pieces of a person's being have been brought together into one whole; in other words, your emotions are not in conflict with your actions, your actions are not in conflict with your ideas. There's been a complete integration of your whole personality. That might be another way of describing enlightenment, or inner revolution, or self-realization, or whatever you want to call it.

G: One's daily life is very different.

A: Yes, because there's no conflict anymore. You see what needs to be done at a certain moment, and if there are no ideas to interfere, the action is performed spontaneously. You do whatever is necessary because you see that it needs doing, so there is no conflict. And the kind of environment which allows you to live this way is created around you. Obviously, if you're living in this way, the kind of an occupation that you follow to earn your living has to harmonize with your lifestyle. For instance, you couldn't work for somebody who demanded that you do things that were in conflict with your inner judgement as to what is right or wrong; it would be impossible. You would have to seek a job in which you had the freedom to spontaneously do the things you perceived to be right. You could no longer lend yourself to actions that you saw to be wrong, actions that did not promote the general well-being of humanity, or that of the rest of the world. It would be impossible.

G: Exactly.

A: I feel that I now live in a state of love, and that has been the major difference that I have noticed in my life. Before all of this happened forty years ago, I loved my wife and I loved my possessions, but in a personal way. I considered them my property. I was very jealous about maintaining the status quo, and all the rest of it. But when this inner transformation happened, there was a great change in my feelings of love; from that time on, I found myself loving everything equally. There was no distinction, from my point of view, between what I called my personal possessions and the outside world. I loved the trees, I loved the birds, I loved the animals, I loved people. I didn't love some of the things other people did, but I realized why they did them. I realized that they were asleep and were doing things in a dreamlike state; they obviously couldn't help themselves, anymore than I had been able to help myself before all of this happened to me.

This gives you a feeling of compassion for other people. You recognize the truth of the saying, "There, but for the grace of God, go I." How true that really is! Because it is only that insight, or that 'otherness' which comes into a person's life uninvited, which enables you to live this kind of a life. We don't know, moment by moment, what is going to happen to us. And it isn't within our power to bring life's sudden challenges about, or to change them. All we can do is prepare the ground and clear the weeds, and 'know' that life is going to take over — eventually bringing the ultimate challenge: death.

G: That compassion flows from you, because I've felt it when someone comes to talk to you. They also feel that you speak from that inner peace and that feeling of compassion for them.

A: That is particularly true if I don't have any preconceptions; if I have any such ideas, it doesn't work at all. Inner peace gives you a feeling of harmlessness. You don't want to harm life. You don't want to go out and cut down a tree that's beautiful; you don't want to cut down anything that's beautiful, and you see beauty wherever you go.

G: It is wonderful.

Now, I'd like to go back to another point for a moment. You said earlier that there is no self-protection, but there must be bodily care; the body needs to be cared for so that you physically have the energy to live in this state of order that we're describing. So it is very important to care for the body, to eat right, and exercise, and get enough sleep, and so on.

A: Yes.

G: If all the conditions we've discussed pertain to enlightenment, what do you consider the main prerequisite for it to flower?

A: I think the bottom line is a quiet mind, as I've said on numerous other occasions. Which raises the following question: how one is to have a quiet mind? Obviously, we can't start out with a quiet mind, can we? The mind is constantly occupied with all kinds of things; even after 'enlightenment' one finds that one's mind is occupied most of the time with reactions to one's conditioning. So you have to explore the subject; you have to be willing to start on the path of self-discovery.

Enlightenment, from my point of view, is not an end result. It is not something that you suddenly achieve, following which you just sit back and experience all the wonders of life. It is only the first step on the return path; it is the birth of intelligence within the very deepest part of one's being. And with that intelligence one begins to explore the world. One begins to explore the worlds beyond thought, as we said before.

G: You begin to resolve some of your conditioning and your reactions to things.

A: You must begin to resolve the residue or conditioning that exists. There has to be a willingness to see it for what it really is, and not apply names to it. When we see that we're jealous we must not be willing to excuse it, justify it, call it by some other name (like 'love'), think a positive rather than a negative thought — we must not be willing to do any of that. You must be willing to just sit there and observe it, be willing to put yourself on the altar of life and say, "All right, life, work your will upon me, whatever it is."

What happens as a result is alchemy; to me it is the real alchemical process. It is a mutation of the conditioned material into its essence, and I feel that the essence becomes a part of universal mind, a part of the process of life, a part of the true reality which lies behind all that we see around us.

G: So enlightenment is a state of insight in the moment.

A: Yes, that's very true. I feel that enlightenment is seeing, moment by moment, the reality of whatever exists at a particular moment, and acting spontaneously and correctly in accordance with that reality rather than in response to some idea. So enlightenment can have nothing to do with ideas, it can have nothing to do with tradition, it can have nothing to do with what we have known in the past, or what we dream up in the future, because it pertains only to the present. If someone says, "I'm enlightened" (which signifies a static state), they are making an incorrect statement. Enlightenment has to involve a moment by moment perception of the clarity and reality of each particular moment, and nothing else.

G: Doesn't that then take you beyond?

A: That is the beyond. It doesn't take you beyond because there is no 'you' in the picture. In seeing something as it is, in seeing the facts as they are, there's no center from which the seeing is done. There's perception, and the perception exists in the beyond. It is the beyond; there's no going beyond. There's no duality in the process at all. That's what is so wonderful about it. There is nothing that you can do consciously in the moment to bring it about; all you can do is to be sure that you're not doing something that prevents it from happening, such as bringing in some egocentric idea or occupation that you might be involved with. It is very simple, so simple that everybody misses it.

Tradition has recognized the phenomenon of enlightenment, but has mistakenly reinforced the belief that it can be experienced through the use of certain techniques or meditation. That approach always proceeds from the known, which is a part of human consciousness.

Enlightenment involves stepping out of the known, into the worlds beyond thought.

HOLISTIC UNDERSTANDING

*When one stops trying to escape from the intense
pain and suffering of a problem, there is
freedom from the known, inviting
holistic understanding.*

G: Al, just what do you mean by holistic understanding?
Are you implying that there are different levels of understanding?

A: I think that it is pretty obvious that there are different
levels of understanding. We can see them at work in our daily
lives, in the occupations that we have, and in whatever else we
do in our daily lives.

G: What do you mean?

A: Well, at a physical level, for instance, we have to learn
how to drive an automobile, and we have to learn how to do
the particular job that we have chosen in order to make a
living. We have to learn how to perform certain actions
physically. don't we?

G: Yes.

A: So that requires understanding at that particular level.

G: It requires technique.

A: We call it technique, but we really mean understanding; understanding how to do something in an efficient way so we can perform a job. At the emotional level, we may either like or dislike our job or our occupation; that's pretty obvious. Some people love their work and do a good job, while other people hate their jobs, and that is reflected in the work that they do. So there is understanding at the emotional level also, isn't there?

G: Yes.

A: We can also intellectually see the value of the work that we do in relationship to ourselves and society, or see the harm that we could possibly do to our society or the world at large. So we can understand these things from an intellectual point of view. At least we assert that we understand them. The man that works at building atomic bombs, for instance, says that he understands his job. He feels that he understands the physical technique involved; he understands his emotional relationship to it; and he intellectually understands it because the government (or whoever it is that is hiring him) has provided him with a rationale, and he believes in it.

But isn't something deeper required? Instead of simply understanding something at these three levels — the levels on which most people live their lives — isn't a deeper level of understanding required in order for someone to be an integrated, intelligent, responsible member of our society?

G: There may be some confusion concerning intellectual understanding and true understanding. Perhaps you could explore that a little more, because many people think they fully understand things.

A: I think that's pretty obvious. For instance, we know people who have been listening to certain religious teachers for many, many years; they feel that they understand those teachers completely, but that understanding is not reflected in their daily lives. In other words, there is a great gap between what they say and what they actually do in the world. That is why I feel that this particular subject is a very vital one. On the surface, it may sound rather uninteresting, it may sound like a topic that we all know about; but I don't think that's true. That's the reason I'd like to explore the subject more fully.

Let's explore the question of what is really meant by holistic understanding. When I use the term, I mean understanding at every level: the physical level, the emotional level, and the mental level, but also the deeper level where all of these are integrated and brought to bear on actual living situations, so that your life is changed by the understanding. That might result in your giving up a particular job, or even doing a better job; it might result in all kinds of things. But the point is that real understanding at this deep level can fundamentally change your life. That's the reason why I feel it is important to investigate this subject in depth.

G: Well, at whatever level one understands, the result is action. Are you suggesting that there are different types of actions as well; that there are incomplete, partial, fragmentary actions like those resulting from the necessity of earning a living? Or are you implying that if there is holistic understanding, there can be true, totally spontaneous action which is also holistic?

A: Let me ask this question: When do we want to understand something? In other words, what conditions occur in life that lead us to want to understand a situation that we find ourselves in?

G: There might be many precursors.

A: I don't think so. Doesn't suffering make me want to understand why I'm suffering, so that I can eliminate the pain? Suffering is one precursor, isn't it?

G: Yes.

A: If I'm in pain, whether it is physical pain or psychological pain, I'm motivated to understand the situation and eliminate the pain, aren't I?

G: It seems so.

A: In other words, suffering (of one kind or another) seems to be an integral part of our daily life, and it is one of the basic motivating forces that gets us to look into ourselves, and look into a situation, in order to bring about a change.

G: Yes.

A: So instead of condemning suffering, instead of trying to escape from suffering, maybe we should welcome it; not by going out and looking for it (since you don't have to look for it), but by trying to examine the situation objectively.

G: Yes.

A: It is always there, and it will come, you know; there's no problem in finding it.

G: As a matter of fact, if you ask for life to bring you deeper understanding, you know what happens!

A: Yes.

G: Many things suddenly begin to happen to you.

A: You're right. So, if that is true — which it seems to be — then the important question is this: At what level are we seeking the understanding needed to alleviate the pain, or the suffering, or the sorrow? Are we seeking it on a physical level alone? Are we seeking it on an emotional level, or on an intellectual level? In other words, are we seeking it on a superficial level, which means that we want to bargain with life: We want to trade this particular suffering for something else, and we'll give this much, we'll do this much, if life will give us so much in return.

G: Yes; at first, one's reaction is always to get rid of the suffering, to eliminate the pain.

A: I feel that that's a natural response; but I also think that suffering is an integral part of living. Perhaps it is in the scheme of things that there should be suffering, because if there wasn't suffering we wouldn't investigate anything. If we were in a pleasant state all of the time, we would never question our values. There would be no changes taking place, there would be no evolutionary growth (or anything else), if everybody was completely happy and satisfied. So perhaps it is something that is inherent and that you can't escape; but you can understand it, and in understanding it, the mental and psychological turmoil is eliminated. You may still suffer physically, but at least you are not fighting it psychologically, which I think intensifies the whole thing.

G: There's nothing quite as effective as suffering physically or hearing a death sentence from a doctor — someone saying that you only have x number of days, weeks, or months to live — in causing a radical change in one's life.

A: That's certainly true.

G: So the first response to suffering is a reaction, and it is merely a desire to change the situation, not to understand it.

A: That brings up another question: What do you think it is that prevents understanding from taking place holistically, rather than superficially? What do you feel are some of the factors that prevent that from happening?

G: Well, one factor was just mentioned: If we simply react to escape suffering, there is no real interest in understanding the basic cause of the pain. We go to someone else to eliminate it: doctors, authorities, our boss at work, our husband, or whoever else we think can help us escape our pain and suffering. We work from the outside inwards. And since our reaction to escape the pain is so strong, we are not even interested in finding out what the cause is.

A: That brings up another question: When can understanding take place? Doesn't it always have to take place in the present moment? You can't understand something in the past;

you can't understand it in the future; it has to be understood right now. Thought always involves an event which happened in the past; understanding has to take place in the present moment. So what is it that keeps us from existing in the present moment? We discussed this before, and came to the conclusion that it seems to be thought and the content of human consciousness — all of our ideas, our opinions, and the conclusions that we come to — that prevent us from living in the present moment. If that is true, how can we catch ourselves actually indulging in, or identifying with, a train of thought at the very moment we should be observing a situation in order to understand it? How can this take place?

G: It seems quite difficult, because if my intention is to escape constant suffering resulting from a situation or a problem, I'm going to use everything that I can; in other words, I'm going to use my whole bag of tricks, everything that's in my field of consciousness, or I'm going to go searching for more knowledge in order to rearrange the facts, or to attack the pain. Again, that's my first reaction. I'll do anything to eliminate that suffering. I'll go on physical exertion programs, and exercise or diet to heal my body. I'll go to an authority who will explain my emotional reactions. I'll go to other authorities who will tell me what to do or think about the pain, or how to live with it and stay happy anyway, etc. I'll go to whoever or whatever is available for help in rearranging and changing, long before I'll sit down and really try to discover why I'm in pain, and have this suffering or sorrow.

A: Perhaps the reaction which you have just described, which seems to be extremely prevalent, is what has kept understanding from progressing beyond the three lowest levels; we have been satisfied with understanding a problem at the physical, emotional, or intellectual levels only. Perhaps that is the reason that humanity hasn't changed fundamentally for many centuries. We have changed our ideas, and we have changed all kinds of other things, but a real change (resulting in a feeling of love and cooperation and responsibility between human beings) hasn't taken place.

G: There are so many people in the world who tell me that they know how to alleviate my suffering.

A: I know, but it is just an idea.

G: There are still other people who tell me how to live with suffering and be happy anyway. And then there are those people who say that it is good to suffer; stay with it; it is the path to gaining *mana,* or sitting next to God, or whatever.

A: Yes, but our acceptance of the explanations or advice that other people give us when we are in these situations keeps our understanding at the lowest levels.

G: Exactly.

A: That's my point. What I'm trying to emphasize is the fact that there is a holistic understanding which surpasses the three lower levels of understanding.

G: So when does someone really want to understand? You asked that question earlier.

A: You want to understand when you are really suffering.

G: Do we always have to be faced with a great crisis and feel that our back is against the wall?

A: I don't think so, but we usually do let it come to that point before we really explore our situation.

G: Yes.

A: Another point to consider is this: When are we willing to give up those concepts? Under what conditions are we unwilling to revert to other people's opinions, other people's advice, or the answers that exist within our own field of consciousness? When are we willing to give them up and actually face a situation at any given moment (which is always the now-moment), without reverting to any of that; under what conditions are we willing to do that?

G: If I see that none of that advice is working, and I'm still suffering, then I become interested in taking responsibility for my own life and any suffering I experience. I stop blaming outside factors or other people for my situation and look at what is really going on, and I'm willing to deal with 'what is': i.e., the reality of the situation.

A: Would you say, therefore, that it is almost mandatory to first try everything that you can think of to alleviate a situation? You try all of your own ideas, you try all of the ideas that other people give you; you try just about everything that you possibly can. In other words, you must be face to face with the situation, with the suffering, with the pain, with the unhappiness, with absolutely no escape from it whatsoever.

G: Then you see that you yourself have to deal with it. No one can do it for you.

A: That's right. Don't we have to be in an almost desperate situation before we can find awareness in the present moment? Any idea or any escape that I've tried in the past is an escape from the present. Any idea that I've acquired from somebody else, that I think will alleviate the situation, prevents me from being aware in the present. They all place me in the realm of thought, away from the present.

If all that is true, then — when you are face to face with a situation which you can't stand, which you don't want to put up with, which you really want to change at a deep level or understand — there can be understanding at that very moment. There can be understanding, a holistic understanding of a situation which goes beyond you. In other words, since you've investigated the physical part of the situation, you've investigated its emotional content, and you've investigated all of the ideas involved in it, you're cleared at those levels, you are free of the known at those levels. You are free of what is known about that particular type of suffering and free of the traditional way of escaping it. And in that freedom from the known, you are face to face with the present moment, face to face with the facts themselves. This brings about an integration, doesn't it? Before, you could say that there was duality: There was you, and there was the idea of how you were going to escape from the situation. There was you, and the opinion that somebody else had provided you with. There was you, and a recognized method of alleviating pain. Therefore, there was always a duality.

G: The recognized methods may help a little bit, may keep me going, may continue my life.

A: Certainly; but that is what everybody is doing, and that is the reason that things don't change fundamentally. Situations are alleviated; we go to an authority and he gives us a new name for a certain situation, and then we usually pay him a great deal of money, but it doesn't actually result in a fundamental change, because as soon as the glamour of the new name has worn off, we're back with our suffering again.

The point I'm trying to emphasize is that holistic understanding means integrated understanding: You and the suffering are one. You are free of the known. Before, the known prevented you from facing the suffering head on; the known prevented you from holistically understanding the situation, but now you are free of it because you have investigated it thoroughly, and it has all turned to ashes in your mouth. You're finally face to face with your pain, and in that confrontation with it as it is, there is a complete integration between you and the suffering. There is no longer 'you' suffering; there is only suffering. Then there can be holistic understanding, which can eliminate the suffering. It may not eliminate the physical part of it, but it eliminates the psychological problems associated with the suffering.

G: Are you saying that you have to go through that each time? You have to be willing to investigate the suffering?

A: I'm not saying you have to; I'm just saying that that seems to be the way things work. That's the way we all behave in the face of suffering. We'll do anything we can to eliminate it. We'll begin with superficial little things — such as changing our environment, or whatever — at the physical level. If that doesn't work, we tackle the emotional aspect. We may go to a psychologist or psychiatrist, or to someone else, for psychological help. Then we explore the situation intellectually. In other words, we do everything but confront the facts. The result is an impasse; all of those things turn to ashes in your mouth, because they are ineffective. Then, and only then, are you actually face to face with the situation, at which time there is a complete integration between you and the suffering, and there is no longer a duality. When there is no duality, holistic understanding can take place. And holistic understanding is not a creation of your self; it is not a part of human consciousness. The other alternatives that you explored were all a part of human consciousness, avenues that humanity has pursued for thousands of years in an attempt to eliminate fear: the fear of death, and of everything else that humanity has been afraid of.

G: I wonder if you aren't leaving out a step here. You suggest that if you stop looking outside of yourself for ways to eliminate a problem which is causing suffering, holistic understanding can occur. I think that there is something more that one has to do: I think that one has to investigate that pain, that suffering, that problem, from an entirely new perspective. You have to let it expose itself. You have to observe what it is that is paining you, without trying to change it, or adjust to it, or discard it, which is difficult. One has to really go into the whole movement of the pain and sorrow and see where it is coming from, because suffering has a way of identifying itself with previous suffering. So one has to look back; do you understand what I'm saying? Let the suffering expose itself; see its relationship to other events in your life; see if there is any meaning to it; see why it is there, how it's come about, and so on. I'm not suggesting that you analyze it, but rather that you stay so aware that you perceive its whole meaning. You can't just say, "I have a pain, I can't do anything," and expect it to leave by itself. It won't. You have to work on it to some extent.

A: Isn't that the upper end of intellectual investigation? In other words, you are pushing your intellectual capacity to look into the situation to the limits.

G: No, I'm not suggesting that you examine it intellectually, or analyze it. I said perceive it; observe it.

A: Yes, but the point we should mention here is that perception is not a part of the thought process; perception is beyond it. Perception is the other factor that can bring about a radical change or transformation.

G: So one should just stay with it, perceive it, be aware of it and all of its implications; just watch it.

A: Yes, but the point is, you can't do that until you have thoroughly investigated all of its other aspects. I'm speaking practically now. Intellectually, perhaps we might not always do so, but I've found that in my own case — and I think this applies to most people — we will try all of the other steps first. We won't go to such lengths immediately. We'll try the simple things, hoping to get out of the situation as easily as possible.

G: Yes.

A: Then, when each of those things have turned out to be ineffective, we are forced more and more into a state of pure perception in which all ideas vanish. In other words, only when there is freedom from the known — the known being all of humanity's ideas — can there be pure perception, in which holistic understanding may take place.

159

G: You must stay with the problem right to the end. You must let it flow and unfold, and show itself to you (which can be very painful), and just watch it. By letting go of what you think about it, the known, each time, a little of the pain goes away; it seems to burn itself out, in a way. That's what I meant by going to the end of it.

A: But I don't think that we can intellectually do it that way. I think that life has to push us farther and farther away from the known before something can happen, and I don't think that you can decide to let it occur. I don't think that it is a conscious decision, because any conscious decision is always in the other direction; the decision is always to escape from pain. So I think you have to have tried everything first. You have to have really tried everything before this process can occur.

If what we have talked about so far is true, let's not waste time thinking that something at a superficial level is going to be really effective in the long run. If you see how superficial such changes must be, then you don't spend too much time on them. Most people are sold on the idea that you can solve the problem of suffering either physically, emotionally, or mentally; they may spend a whole lifetime spinning their wheels and never escaping it. But if you or I have seen the fallacy of this course of action, or how ineffective it really is, then we might spend a little bit of time on it, but we won't spend our whole lifetime on it. We'll go from one thing to another rather quickly, and arrive at the point where there is freedom from the known, at which time this integrated, holistic understanding can take place. Isn't that true?

G: Yes.

A: Everything depends upon your level of maturity.

G: I think that you're now raising the point that there is another approach. You're saying that it is possible to just stay with your suffering and pain, looking at it and letting it show you where it is coming from, and as it unfolds, it will drop away. It is like peeling an onion; if you take off layer after layer, by the time you come to the bottom or center of it, there might be nothing left.

A: I think that raises the following question: Can we catch ourselves reverting to a preconceived explanation or idea, when we are face to face with a situation which requires understanding?

G: Possibly.

A: It seems to be a pretty difficult thing to do, because when we are in the midst of the battle, so to speak, we are so caught up in it, so identified with it, that it is difficult to be objective. But I think that we must realize beforehand that all philosophies, all opinions, all explanations, all authorities (including ourselves) are what furnish us with the ideas which we superimpose between ourselves and the situation. If we realize that ahead of time, and have seen the danger in it, there is a possibility of catching ourselves in the process of doing this.

G: Then the pain itself can be the red light, the danger signal.

A: Yes, the pain can act as an alarm clock to wake us up. I think that at least you have to have seen the logic of this; that is, you have to have seen the logic in the fact that if you superimpose an idea, or a philosophy, or an opinion, or someone else's authority (even your own) between you and the suffering, you are automatically creating a dual situation — there is duality. There is you and the idea, the suffering and the idea, all of which is a part of a dual process, and there can be no holistic understanding when dualism exists. If you can comprehend that beforehand, at least intellectually, then when the alarm clock of suffering rings, or an uncomfortable situation arises, there's a possibility that you can catch yourself reverting to one of these explanations. Then, in that realization, in the integration of that moment, there can be insight into the situation and an understanding at a deeper level that clarifies it so that it will never return. There is no postponement of it, there is no substitution of a positive thought for a negative one, or anything like that. There is an actual elimination of that particular problem, because you have completely understood it at a very deep level.

G: It is the 'I' that suffers, it is the ego that suffers, it is my content of consciousness, my image of myself that suffers, that feels the pain. What is it that sees that there is another approach to that pain?

A: In the first place, what do we call pain? Pain can exist on several different levels. There is physical pain, which can be a natural result of some indiscretion on our part, involving perhaps something in our diet, the way we live, our lifestyle, or whatever; or it can be a consequence of some hereditary malfunction in our system, resulting from the fact that one of our ancestors transgressed the laws of nature and didn't live according to the order of life. So we might be born with a body that is susceptible to pain. But I think it is psychological pain that must be understood.

Would you say that psychological pain stems from the realization that life has just presented us with a bill for something, some diversion or amusement that we wanted? As I said the other day, life is like a big department store, and you can have anything that you want; all of our desires have a pricetag, but usually it is not apparent, or we don't even look at it. We don't want to. We are so enamored by the product that we wish to acquire that we don't even want to look at the price. So you might say that the psychological pain associated with these things occurs when the payment comes due. You suddenly get a bill in the mail that you hadn't even thought about. You thought your acquisition was free, but suddenly you get a bill and have to pay for it.

G: Yes. Psychological pain seems to depend completely on my desires: "I want this," and if I get it I'm happy, but if I don't get it there's pain. That's the bottom line.

A: Yes. So haven't we determined that direct perception is necessary at the moment something is occurring in order for there to be understanding? There has to be direct perception; there can't be any bringing in of ideas or conclusions ahead of time, or anything like that. There has to be direct perception, which involves freedom from the known, freedom from the past, freedom from the ideas that we have; and in that direct perception, holistic understanding occurs. I don't see it as being part of 'me'; I don't feel it is a part of human consciousness. It is an understanding which comes from direct perception.

Another point which stands out is that there has to be an actual experiencing of the suffering, doesn't there? You can't simply have an idea about it. In other words, if you are not suffering right at this moment, but you are trying to solve your suffering right at this moment, the only thing that you can do is intellectualize about it. You must wait until life actually confronts you with the situation again (which it will do); that's because if you haven't solved a certain situation and it is a part of your conditioning, life is going to bring it to your attention over and over again, until you finally face it.

G: It will replay.

A: There will be a continual replay all of the time. So you can't just investigate something intellectually. As we mentioned the other day when we talked about exploring Russia or some other country intellectually; you don't actually do it. So I don't think that you have to worry about a situation reoccurring; if it is a part of you, it will replay itself on some future occasion, and then your complete attention will be required at that moment if you're going to understand it.

G: In a crisis situation, the emotional content may be so overwhelming that one is incapable of looking, watching, or perceiving it with any objectivity.

A: If you are observing the facts of the case, if you have freed yourself from the known escapes from that particular situation in which you are involved, and have seen that you can't do anything about it, then I think that in that moment of not knowing, the cup is empty; your personal psychological cup is empty and something else can come into it. I think that something else is intelligence.

G: But the 'I' wants to do something about the situation. The whole struggle stems from the fact that the 'I' wants to do something about it. And the moment you suggest to me that I cannot do anything about a problem, the pain increases; the crisis seems to be much worse; the flames go higher. My back is completely against the wall if you tell me that I cannot do anything about a problem by using what I already know.

A: I'm not saying that you cannot do anything about a problem; you have to find out that *you* can't do anything about it. If there is some idea in your mind that you can do something about it, for God's sake go for it, do it, and let it turn to ashes in your mouth. That is what we all do most of the time.

G: I'm starting to recognize that. The minute I begin to perceive that I cannot do anything about a problem, it seems to become overwhelming. But perhaps I have to persevere with that feeling, and know that I cannot manipulate it any more. That creates a kind of energy, and a willingness to look at the pain and see where it is coming from and follow it until I can get to the source. In other words, I must let it burn itself out. There is a moment there where I have to be willing to move with the pain, and take a new direction with it.

A: The point I'm trying to emphasize is that this is not done on the conscious level. I don't believe that it can be planned. When I look back on my own past life, and remember being in these kinds of crises, I see that I would have escaped in any way that I possibly could. I don't think that you can consciously say, "All right, I'm going to face this, I'm going to put aside all of my escapes, I'm going to put aside all of my ideas." You can't consciously do that, because when your back is against the wall you are going to try everything possible. It is only when life has pushed you to extremities that you are going to face your problem. It is not a matter of being willing to face it; you *are* facing it, because there is nowhere else you can go, since you have tried absolutely every other escape possible. I think it is that feeling of utter helplessness which creates the fear that we can't face the pain. We know that we can't face it on our own. We've tried everything. We feel completely unable to confront the situation, and that causes fear, and engenders the knowledge — the intuitive, instinctive knowledge — that we don't have the energy to cope with the situation. It is that feeling of inadequacy that leads us to seek help, isn't it? We go to someone else for consolation — we go to a psychologist, a psychiatrist, or whoever we can for advice — because we instinctively know that we can't face the situation ourselves, that we don't have what it takes to do so. Isn't that true?

G: Yes.

A: So, this is really putting yourself on the altar of life and letting life work its will on you, isn't it?

G: Yes, it is.

A: But we are not doing it consciously. We are not saying, "All right, life, work your will on me." We are not doing that, but that is actually what is happening. We are on the altar of life. We are being fried to a crisp in our suffering, and we don't have the energy to do anything about it. And it is in that extremity that the alchemical process takes place.

G: What do you mean?

A: Holistic understanding occurs. Intelligence is born. Our holistic understanding of the situation produces energy, which comes from some source outside of ourselves and the situation

is faced. We don't die on the altar of life, we aren't extermi-
nated, we don't come to a complete end, we aren't reduced to
a condition of complete nothingness. An inner transformation takes place instead. The butterfly emerges from the
cocoon. That apparently is what happens, but the point is that
we can't consciously do this; you can't decide to do this ahead
of time. All you can do is investigate all of the escapes that
you have always used in the past to extricate yourself from
problems, and when you find them ineffective, then (and only
then) can you confront the situation. Then, perhaps, holistic
understanding will take place, although it may not. If you
have even the slightest idea that you are doing it for this purpose, it is another escape. You must see that you can't bargain
with the problem at all; there must be no bargaining. All that
you can do is to let your curiosity, your innate instinct for
questioning and inquiry, carry you to the point where something can really happen to you.

G: Yes.

A: Doesn't that bring about true understanding? And if you
experienced that process at least once in connection with some
small, minor problem, wouldn't it really be the beginning of
faith?

G: An inner knowing that there is another way . . .

A: You might call it faith; you might also call it trust, for
example. If a person was religiously inclined, they might say it
is faith in God, or faith in life, a faith that there is something
beyond the grasp of the human intellect — something that
can step in, and does step in, when we've done our utmost to

alleviate a situation and nothing that we've done is effective. Then, and only then, can something else happen; and when it does, it is the origin of faith, isn't it? If I jump off a high building and experience firsthand the results of the law of gravity by having my body smash into the ground at the end of the fall, I will certainly acquire a certain kind of faith, won't I? I will have faith in the law of gravity, at the very least!

G: And that's outside of the field of consciousness also.

A: Of course, it all is. You know, I think that faith is an interesting thing, because I feel that it is something that most people lack, especially in this materialistic, scientific age that we live in. I think people lack faith.

G: The thought process doesn't engender faith.

A: I think that point might be worth exploring a little: That is, how does faith come about? How is faith born in our lives?

G: Well, let's back up a minute. A lot of people would say that they have faith in their own intellectual capacity; that's where they put their faith. They function entirely through the intellect, and it brings them a certain sense of security; they have a faith in their knowledge.

A: The scientist has faith in his science; the biologist, for example, has faith in biology.

G: Most people have faith in themselves, because they know that their minds can solve the problems of life up to a certain point, or at least until they encounter a situation where there is so much pain and suffering that nothing works.

A: That's right. Would you say that perhaps insight is the first step? We have all had insights from time to time, haven't we? You could call them sudden inspirations; you could call them clear seeing; but we have all had such insights, probably daily. We have insights even in small things. But what do we usually do with an insight that we get? What happens to it on most occasions? It goes around and around in the mind, doesn't it? Instead of converting the insight into direct action, we engage in mental gymnastics. We justify our failure to follow the insight that we have just had, and give reasons for not doing so. We say, "Well, I don't have time to do it right now. I have a job, I'm involved in this or that, and I can't pursue it now." We justify our inaction, draw conclusions about it, and so on.

For example, people have been listening to Krishnaji for many, many years. They will go and hear the man — or any other great teacher for that matter, it doesn't have to be Krishnaji — they will go and listen to him, and get carried away by his personality, by something that they feel is there; they feel an otherness, an 'other' quality about him. And they agree with what he is saying at that moment, because they are carried away by the strength of his conviction at that moment. And perhaps they decide on the way home that they are going to pursue the particular insight that they had; they are going to live a different kind of a life. They are going to endeavor to put into practice what they had seen to be true. But, then what happens? They start analyzing it, they start figuring out the pros and cons: Is this going to get me something, is it going to cost me something? If I actually put this into practice, what are my friends going to think about it; what's my family going to think about it? Is it going to be detrimental to my job or my position in life? And so the energy that was created — the energy that is innate, that is inherent in the insight — is dissipated in the thought process, isn't it?

G: Yes, just so.

A: So they don't convert the insight into actual practice. It doesn't come down onto the physical plane as an action, and so no faith is born, is it? There is no faith in that kind of incomplete action.

G: No.

A: So you can listen to Krishnaji or you can listen to somebody else, for year after year after year, and nothing will happen in your life. We ourselves have seen this over and over again. We know many people who are in this position. They can quote Krishnaji forever, and they know all the answers.

G: Or they can quote Jesus, or the Buddha; you know, you can't blame the teacher for the inadequacy of the student.

A: Exactly.

G: But you were asking about insight, which we talked about the other day; it seems to me that whenever there is a small clarity, a medium-size insight, or a very big insight in a crisis situation, it creates its own energy; it creates its own light. And that energy is what then brings about a transformation, a change, a resolving of your suffering or problem.

A: True, but what I was saying just now is that the energy is there in the original insight.

G: Yes.

A: And that energy is usually dissipated in self-centered thought: What will I personally gain or lose?

G: Yes, that can happen.

A: If it is not dissipated in the thought process, the insight is sometimes so strong, and the conviction so strong, that it results in an act of heroism. There is direct action. And the moment that you see that something has to be done and you do it, you are serving as a channel for life in that action, aren't you? As we were saying the other day, you are acting as a channel for an energy which is not of your own making, and you're bringing that energy down onto the physical plane. But in so doing, you are only a channel. You are engaged in what I call holistic action, and it brings about a holistic understanding at a profound level.

Holistic understanding could be another name for faith, couldn't it? Because once you've done something holistically — once you've performed a holistic action — you know you took the right action. Most people at some time in their lives have done something like this. They've acted spontaneously, either because they saw it was right, or because they didn't have any other choice; everything happened so quickly that their thought process couldn't enter in and interfere with the response. The ego had to stand aside for the moment, although it probably intruded later during the replay or editing of the action by the mind, which produced a memory of the situation. But at the actual moment of the action there was direct action. And there was energy in that; there was understanding in that; there was holistic understanding at a very profound level. Inwardly, you realize that this occurred; you might not be able to consciously act upon it again, but inwardly you know that you acted correctly.

G: Yes, you can again open the door to that inner knowing.

A: The more often that this can be done, the more often

you are acting as a channel for life, and in that there is a holistic understanding of life. Then you realize inwardly that you yourself as an ego are nothing. You may use your thoughts and ideas as tools, but they don't rule your life. Something else is ruling your life, something outside of yourself. You then become a worker for the world; you help the world. You contribute to the situation in which you find yourself. Your relationships with your family, your friends, and with everybody else are the right kinds of relationships.

G: So you are saying that when you open the door for a new look at yourself, insight may occur, which brings understanding in a complete, holistic way; that in turn resolves the pain and the suffering and brings about direct action, and from that faith is born: a faith in life.

A: Right. The point that I'm trying to emphasize is that none of the good things in life — love, compassion, friendship, honesty, integrity, holistic understanding — are separate entities. They are all a part of this innate intelligence which rules the world, and of which you and I can be a conscious part when our cup is empty, when we are free of the known, free of the content of human consciousness. We are able to use it as a tool, but we are free of it when we don't need to use it. When we are free of that, our cup is empty, and an otherness can flow into it. This otherness contains everything. It contains understanding; it contains the solution to all problems. It engenders a healing process within us. It regenerates each of us. You find that all of the little faults and shortcomings that you had begin to evaporate in the light of intelligence. You find changes taking place within you that are not stemming from your ego. You're not willing yourself to be better, you're not thinking about being more and more virtuous or whatever. But there is a transformation in your inward state so that what you manifest to the outer world is a reflection of the inward changes brought about by intelligence.

G: Perhaps the most positive thing that we can do in order to live this way — to live the different kind of life that we were talking about the other day — is to continually lay aside the known, shed the thought process. Use it when it is necessary, but lay it aside when it is inefficient, when we see that it doesn't help us to resolve our problems. The more you can lay thought aside, the more you can open the door to holistic understanding.

A: But it is important to recognize that you can't consciously put thought aside; it simply drops away at the moment of awareness, and intelligence then sees the right action to take. I think the first step that one must take is to see (at least intel-lectually) that what I'm describing is true, and you can't do that without experimentation. You have to be willing to ex-periment with your own life; you have to be willing to try things. Don't accept anyone as an authority; realize that you, and only you, can really understand what life is all about. When you do that, you're open to this otherness. All that you or I can do is wake up and be attentive. You can't consciously awaken yourself, but if you have cleared the ground, cleared away the weeds, cleared away as much of the known as you can, it can happen.

G: You must see the necessity of doing that.

A: Yes, then it can happen. You can't consciously awaken yourself, but it can happen, it can occur. And that is what really brings about the radical inner transformation that Krishnaji and some of the other great teachers have talked about.

If we have the capacity for direct action following insight, then faith (which may be called holistic understanding) is born. Insight has an energy which can solve all problems, an energy which doesn't diminish with ill health, or anything else. That energy creates a holistic life in which there is no conflict. There are no psychological problems carried over from the past, because you confront them as they come up; you face them with direct perception, and not with ideas. Then, there is an end to suffering and the start of a holistic life.

PART II

THREE LETTERS

The following letters are only a few of many written by Albert Blackburn on the subject of now-consciousness. However, he felt that these specific examples were particularly clear, and would answer many of the questions that were addressed to him. For this reason, these letters were sent out whenever he felt it to be appropriate.

Dear M.:

Thank you for your letter; it was good to hear from you again. You asked, "What is faith; is there a faith which is not faith in an idea, in another person, or in ourselves, but which is a faith unsustained by any idea within human consciousness?"

If true faith does exist, it must spring from some source, from something real, something beyond the manipulation of the thought process. My own feeling is that faith is a result, and therefore cannot be sought directly as a goal.

In looking into this myself, I've concluded that lack of faith seems to be a common problem for many people. For example, thousands of people have listened to Krishnaji for years, but little has actually changed in their everyday relationships. They go to the talks, read the books, and discuss their understanding of his teachings with their friends. How much of this is translated into direct action in their lives? It becomes just another belief system, unless it is brought down to the physical plane through action.

It seems to me that the foundation from which all true things arise is love. Love is affection for truth, the truth in this case being the totality of each moment. Through perception, using all of my senses, I have the capacity to understand my relationship with this truth. In that moment to moment understanding, right action is perceived, and that is insight.

I feel that that is the critical moment. What do I do with the understanding or insight that I have perceived? Do I act immediately, or do I drop into the thought process, which I can use to safely evaluate and analyze the problem? Engaging the brain in rationalization brings in ideas of time, fear, greed, and self-interest, as well as the inner knowledge that I am personally responsible for both the action and its results. Involving insight in this type of rationalization dispels the original energy that was inherent in my understanding and insight.

In the beginning there is a feeling of great energy, energy enough to see me through the required action, but if I allow it to become entangled in the thought process it is dissipated, and I am left with only a memory. Deep down inside, I know that I have somehow missed an opportunity. I feel that it is the accumulation of these psychological memories that prevents me from direct action. However, if the insight is very clear, and the energy within it is overwhelming, I am able to bypass my conditioning and act directly; this completes the circuit, which is grounded in right action. The energy contained in insight requires direct action on my part. This brings with it a feeling of well-being, inner peace, and the knowledge that I have objectively done my best; for in this type of action there is no self-recrimination, no matter what the outcome. I have not acted, life has acted through me.

I feel that this is the beginning of faith. It is the natural outcome of direct action: action in which the calculating ego was temporarily in abeyance. That type of action may only happen occasionally, but each time it does faith is strengthened, and it becomes easier. If you can experience the reality of this, then awareness will alert you moment to moment as to what type of action you are involved in: direct action, or delayed action.

You begin with an awareness of how clever the mind is. If you have faith only in thought, you can justify any delayed action and thereby turn the creative energy of insight into the burden of psychologial memory. But in direct action there is no psychological memory; instead, there is a faith which contains peace, love, honesty, unselfishness, well-being, cooperation, harmony, joy, and a feeling of unity.

Don't let this remain an idea! Try it and see what happens.

With much affection,

Al Blackburn

Dear H.:

Thank you for your letter; I hope that I can answer your questions to your satisfaction.

Your main question, which recurs throughout your letter, concerns insight and who or what it is that acts. I think that Krishnaji has answered this very clearly in his recent book Exploration Into Insight, but here are my own personal views, very briefly stated.

Every happening in the ceaseless flow of life occurs moment by moment; each one is complete, with no continuity. My perception of any event is instantaneous, and can be called insight. My brain is a product of the evolutionary process and of time. My brain is incapable of seeing or evaluating the flow of events because they are out of time, and my brain can only recognize events that are reconstructed by my limited consciousness through the time process. That inability of my brain to capture the fleeting moments of reality has led to what I call a 'replay' mechanism. I feel that there must be many sincere followers of Krishnaji's teachings who have tried to watch their thoughts, instead of watching the movement of thought.

If you carefully watch what happens, you will see that non-directive observation cannot occur at the same time as thought. There is either one or the other; the two cannot occur simultaneously. In order to cope with its own inadequacies, the brain has set up an 'instant replay system' so that live happenings, thoughts, and actions can be reviewed and thereby brought into the field of individual consciousness. This gives you the feeling that you (your ego) are in control.

You can alter the reviewed material in various ways; you can add to it, judge it, condemn it, etc. The results of this mental activity comprise the content of consciousness. It is from that content that all of your self-centered activities originate, but you believe that you are responding directly to challenges!

There are several difficulties involved in understanding this. First, you must doubt the validity of the replay process. Second, it must be seen in action, rather than as an idea or in replay. Third, you cannot rely on anything within the field of consciousness, because that material is all time-related, and each event within any given moment is out of time. Fourth, your thought process, the ego, demands to be in control; that is the reason that this whole process has acquired such momentum since it first began. Actually, of course, you have no control over events.

Now suppose that someone like Krishnaji comes along and questions the whole process: Here is a real threat to everything you ever thought was true! If the situation can be faced without escape, the result can be a radical inner transformation, involving the death of the ego. The thought process can no longer be relied upon to sustain self-centered thought and activities.

Everything you know or can think about stems from the content of consciousness. The tendency to react in the old, established ways is almost overwhelming, but the habit can be overcome, not by a conscious endeavor on your part, but by non-directional observation. This elicits the help of insight and Intelligence functioning through awareness. As Krishnaji said, "Goodness can only flower outside the field of time" — your consciousness is entangled with time.

I feel that many sincere followers of Krishnaji — in trying to follow his instructions — mistake their sudden awareness of what they have just been thinking for the observance of thought. The fundamental change of consciousness that Krishnaji speaks of is only possible through a non-directive awareness at the exact moment of occurrence. That takes place outside of the time-binding activity of consciousness as you know it.

That is the only real transformation or regeneration of the material within your field of consciousness that is possible, and there is unlimited energy associated with it. The energy which you ordinarily use contains conflict and contradiction, and slowly fades away with ill health, disease, and old age. A failure to act upon the insights resulting from non-directional observation short-circuits this energy, and you are back again in your field of consciousness with only your replay mechanism left, a mechanism that you might mistake for the real thing.

You asked the question, "What is it that decides to take action?" It is your ego (your thought process) that makes all decisions, and that is a part of the dualistic process of thought. Any decision entails a choice between alternative courses of action. Direct action, springing from insight, arises when you see all the related facts at the moment. In that complete perception there is no decision necessary, and hence no duality.

In the beginning, due to the habit-energy involved, you are again and again carried away by the thought process that is triggered by memory, when life confronts you with something that corresponds to some past event. Because those past events were only partially met, through the two-dimensional replay mechanism, they were stored in your memory; and that is how you continue to meet the ever-changing challenges of life. But once you become aware of what is happening, you can never be completely satisfied with that whole process; as a result of your inner intention to face life directly, you can begin the "return path."

Do not get trapped into looking for any result or goal, as

that is part of old habits of thought, and will prevent the actual regeneration from working. There will be many times when pure perception is there, leading to direct action, and many times when the old reasserts itself; all you can do is your best, moment by moment, with no thought of reward.

When direct action goes along with observation, Intelligence is acting. When action takes place after a mental replay, it is the old ego that is acting. The moment of *now* is multidimensional and contains the life element necessary to bring about an instant transformation and a complete understanding of any event. Any replay, on the other hand, is only two-dimensional, and therefore does not lead to understanding and freedom. It is like taking a movie of something and then rerunning the film in the privacy of your home in order to delete certain frames and retouch others; the finished, edited version is placed in your personal memory bank for use when life presents a similar challenge. That edited material is both the personal and collective content of your consciousness.

Whenever a situation is only partially met at the moment of its occurrence, the memory of it is stored in the brain. That material is what triggers thought to rerun or replay the scene over again. We have been led to believe that we can be free of this material through analysis or some other type of mental manipulation, but I feel that it is only suppressed. I have found that the memory replay will recur until I am able to meet a similar event (which life *will* bring) directly at the moment it happens. The old residue is dissolved in the light of insight, and I am free of the replay memory concerning that particular event.

As Krishnaji said, "Truth is a pathless land and no one but yourself can point out the way." It is consciousness, made up of the residue of incomplete experiences in the past, that prevents you from meeting the challenges of life factually. If you really see this (with all its implications), then the next logical step is to be free of all that content. Consciousness, as you know it, is the ego and all the intricacies of the thought process.

I feel that there can be no motive, goal, or reward in your inner intention to experiment, in your new approach to life. You must come to it through an elimination of all the known escapes. Only when every possible way out of your dilemma has proved fruitless will you be willing to discard the known and face the unknown. Nothing else can be done. What takes place then is a radical inner transformation.

This transformation probably differs in depth and quality, depending on the person involved, but I feel that it does involve the activation of new brain cells. It has been said by some brain specialists that most of us only use about one-tenth of our total brain capacity. The part that we do use is involved in dealing with the world in which we live, and in relating to our particular environment. That environment, which we have learned to recognize and name, differs in location, climate, and population. It is a fact that the brain must have security if it is to develop normally, and it finds its security in being able to name and thereby establish a relationship with its environment. That naming process is handed down from generation to generation through education, and through the medium of the prevailing culture in which we live. We are taught to recognize and name everything, which gives us a sense of inward security. All of this is obviously necessary up to a certain point, but if you are to go beyond the level of mere physical existance, a radical change in your perspective must occur.

As long as you are satisfied with things as they are, or as they appear to be, you will follow the accepted pattern. There must come a time when you begin to question all of the values that you have accepted as important. Those values, in many cases, are a result of the recognition process. In other words, you do not directly apprehend the environment in which you live; instead, you live in a world of recognized values, the products of humanity's reactions to the environment since time began. This is consciousness as you know it. It is a product of time and space, and it is within these limited parameters of conditioning that your brain has developed its present capacities to respond to the ever-changing challenges of life.

You are constantly being challenged by something over which you have no control. You cannot always predict what you are going to do or what you are going to say, let alone what greater surprises may lie in wait for you day by day. Your brain simply cannot cope with such uncertainty, so it has developed the thought process to explain and name these ever-changing events. If you are aware of the limits of the thought process, you see that you can only think of one thing at a time. Obviously, each event in life contains many factors and has a complex structure whose intricacies cannot be captured by thought.

You are used to meeting the events of everyday life with thought; that is the recognition process. You miss the actual events as they occur, moment by moment, but you have set up the replay mechanism to slow the process down so that you can recognize enough details to give it all some semblance of logic. You pick out specific details according to your past conditioning, and from all of this you fashion the fabric of your consciousness.

If this is true, you can see how limited your life and the consciousness in which all your thinking takes place must be. You can expand your consciousness through education and by broadening your scope of activities, but it will remain what it is: the product of time and space.

The only way out of this impasse is moment to moment

awareness. This is cognition — or pure perception — before recognition occurs. Then you are in direct contact with the event itself, and new brain cells are activated in the process; old cells are in abeyance, as they only function in time and space. The present moment is outside of time and space, and therefore occurs outside of consciousness as you know it.

As I have said, the present moment is multidimensional and contains all of the life qualities necessary for complete understanding. If one can meet the present without the burden of the past, memory is not involved and the thought process is not triggered. The result of that attention to each moment is a total regeneration of the human psyche at many levels. That is the real meaning of transformation. It always exists in the *NOW* of each moment, outside of consciousness; therefore, regeneration is unrecognizable while it is actually taking place. Recognition always occurs within consciousness as you know it.

Actually, you spend your life in two worlds: the factual world of everyday events, and the inner world of personal consciousness. You exist in a state of dualistic reactions rather than one of integrated action. You must, of course, begin wherever you find yourself. All values must be questioned, not blindly accepted. Thought must be used in dealing with the phenomenal world, but you must be psychologically free to explore the fascinating worlds beyond thought, using the new faculty of Intelligence. That Intelligence is awakened when you step out of the confines of your limited consciousness and step into the world of reality, without the burden of the past. That can only happen *NOW!*

I hope this brings some clarity for you.

Affectionately,

Al Blackburn

Dear R.:

Thank you for your letter. I will answer your questions by sending you this parable which I wrote in 1974, entitled The Train of Thought.

* * *

One day I awakened to find myself standing on the platform of a railway station. The platform was crowded with the entire human race, and everyone but me (I somehow knew) was sleepwalking. I did not know what had awakened me, or what had led me there; I did know that I was awake and apparently could see the real meaning of what was happening around me.

In that most unusual state in which I found myself, I was able to see many strange and wonderful things that no one else could apparently see. Each person on the platform was enclosed in an aura resembling a soap bubble of many colors, and each color, I knew, represented their qualities and interests. There were no two exactly the same, but people did seem to gravitate into groups having similar colors.

The station building itself, where tickets were sold, was a beehive of activity. There were numerous signs advertising such different destinations as Self-Fulfillment, Peace, War, Religion, and so on; the possibilities seemed unlimited. In a few cases the price of the ticket was clearly marked, but in most it was not. No one seemed interested in what a trip would cost, as long as the ticket could be paid for later, or charged on a credit card. There was a sign saying that all sales were final; no refunds or exchanges were possible once the trip was taken.

There were many authorities present acting as guides, teachers, and advisors. They were clearly identified by their dress and by the rather prominent badges that they wore. I could see that most of the prospective passengers were so carried away by the whole procedure that without someone's help they would have indiscriminately climbed aboard the first car to appear. Others, of a more discriminating nature, eagerly sought advice from the authority that appealed to them the most.

Many authorities went out of their way to recruit gullible passengers, and in this way were able to build up quite a reputation. Word was passed from generation to generation through tradition, which was thought to be the best authority of all to follow.

I myself had always preferred to make my own choice, and therefore had never followed the advice of any of these well-known authorities. I found out later that it was my independent attitude that had led to my present state of wakefulness on the platform. I saw that accepting any authority was an absolute guarantee that one would never awaken, and without awakening, there was an endless trip through space and time.

The whole scene was intensely interesting to me as I watched what seemed to be happening. Some people got on board and were not seen again, while others would jump on, only to get off almost immediately. There seemed to be no rules of behavior, since some passengers kept changing cars and even seats for reasons known only to themselves.

The track leading in and out of the station was only visible for a short distance in either direction, for the train entered a tunnel immediately after leaving the boarding area. The arriving train (which I now saw was only a continuation of the same train) also emerged from a tunnel just before its arrival at the station. I was unable to determine the length of the train, but I could see that it was continuous. It was also unique in a most peculiar way — there were five distinct types of railway cars, each with its respective color, shape, size, and different way of attracting my attention. For a time I was puzzled by this, but I finally saw a signboard with a description that enabled the passengers to make a choice. The first car listed on the sign was called The Car Of Sight, the second The Car Of Sound, the third The Car Of Touch, the fourth The Car Of Taste, and the fifth The Car Of Smell. This information, of course, explained many things to me, and I again focussed my attention on this fantastic train.

As I watched the people around me, I could see that they were apparently caught up in a ceaseless round of activity. They behaved in much the same way that a person does when under hypnosis. Their attention was focused entirely on the train, and they seemed to be unaware of anything else. A constant loading and unloading was going on, and for a time I was at a loss as to why a certain car was chosen. Finally I perceived that each person's choice was motivated by a subtle blending of interests, familiarity, prejudice, fear, and desire. The blending of these qualities in a person was expressed by an overall tone or frequency, which in some corresponding way was linked to a tone or similar frequency that was emitted by each car as it passed by. The result apparently was like a post-hypnotic suggestion in its effect on the prospective passengers. As I watched people's reactions, I was struck more and more by the dreamlike quality of the scene.

All of this time, I was in a state of wakefulness in which I could watch the proceedings with detached interest. But now I also wanted to experience this fascinating train ride that everyone else seemed to be enjoying so much. The instant my decision to participate was made, a subtle change in my own perception occurred. My attention was immediately drawn to what seemed to me to be the most beautiful car, which was just arriving. I barely had time to get on board, but found to my delight that it had unlimited seating capacity. Every seat individually molded itself to each passenger and automatically adjusted to suit that person's tastes and mental attributes.

Before sitting down in my own choice seat, I glanced around me and saw a glassy look in the eyes of all the seated passengers. My own eyes no doubt took on the same trance-like look, because as I sat down all memory vanished along with my objective perception. I too was lost in my own private dream world, and I was so busy correlating this new experience with my past life that time just seemed to disappear. By the time this assimilation had taken place, I realized that I must be missing the thrill of riding in other cars. I jumped off on the platform and immediately awakened again to the world around me, and realized that I had been asleep and dreaming.

The rest of that day I spent experimenting. I would take different cars and different seats, but the result was always the same. I found that as long as I remained on the platform a clear perception of everything could be maintained, but the moment that my attention was arrested by an unusually attractive car I would fall asleep, and everything experienced from that point on was a part of my own personal dream-world, and in a rather vague way was connected to that of the other passengers in my general group. Of course, I had many interesting discussions with my fellow travelers on science, religion, and philosophy, and we reassured one another that some of the rather frightening things that happened were either necessary or happened through the will of God.

It was only after I had jumped off that my memory would return, and I could remember all of the events leading up to the moment when my attention had been diverted, and recall the very subtle way in which my choice of cars and seats had been influenced. I could also remember everything that I had experienced while on the train, and even the supposedly intelligent conversations which had taken place in the cars. While I remained on the platform, in an objective state, I could see how superficial our lengthy discussions had been. What had seemed to be the whole world had only been a tiny fragment of it, so that any judgement or action stemming from it accomplished very little good. The complete picture could be seen and intelligent action taken only by remaining on the platform and in the state of awareness.

I also saw that even though the cars of Sight, Sound, Touch, Taste, and Smell were separate, they were all part of the same train, and were only focal points that attracted attention. Once on board, a mysterious blending of the whole dream-train into a single unity took place. A kind of mutual conditioning effect occurred: The passengers took on the qualities of the train, and the train took on the qulities of its passengers. I could see that this gradual conditioning process — called by some growth, progress, or evolution —was only a sort of glorified "merry-go-round."

I could see the whole picture only by stepping off the train. It was easy to be caught up in the mass hysteria, especially as no advance payment had to be made for a ride; anyone could jump on board. Many, no doubt, thought there was a free trip to an ultimate pleasure, and were unaware that it was a "pay as you leave" system. Some of the prices paid seemed to me to be extremely high, since they included sickness, old age, and death; naturally, there was a great deal of grumbling when payment fell due.

After a great deal of inquiry, I found out that there had been other, isolated cases similar to mine, in which individuals had awakened, and because it did happen from time to time, a new type of pass had been authorized. It was called "The Cycle Of Perception," and was available free of charge to anyone with the capacity for awareness.

I immediately took advantage of this information and obtained one of these special passes, and from then on my experience was quite different. Instead of falling asleep immediately, and remaining asleep for the duration of the trip, I only slept at the moment of choice; immediately thereafter I was able to wake up, and the rest of the trip took place in a state of awareness.

It seemed to work in the following way: As the cars came into view, and I began to feel an irresistable attraction towards a particular car, I would fall asleep; I would then awaken in my favorite seat on that car. I had always remained asleep for the duration of the trip when this had happened before, but now I was able to watch the whole procedure objectively in a waking state. I could see the superficiality of the whole scene, and was no longer carried away by the conversations of my fellow passengers. In this way, my desire to blindly participate in this means of transportation gradually diminished, and as a consequence my trips became shorter and less frequent.

The use of "The Cycle Of Perception" pass was mandatory during the transition that I was going through, a transition from a state of unconscious participation (in which I was immersed in a hypnotic dream) to a state of complete wakefulness (in which there was no longer any desire to use this antiquated means of transportation).

I have since tried to tell others on the platform of my experiences, but my words seem to fall on deaf ears. Some people think I'm crazy, but most think that even questioning such a wonderful train system is foolish. "It is here, so why not enjoy it," they say. Others think that I should not speak about it, for fear that some authority might overhear and bring the whole thing to an end. Personally, I am tired of watching this "merry-go-round," and keep wondering if it may not all vanish into thin air some day. How and why it originally got started is a mystery, but its continuity is assured through the unlimited supply of avid passengers recruited from the entire human species.

In closing my account of the strange phenomenon which I have been describing, let me add the following. I have found out that this train was conceived of and dedicated millions of years ago by the earliest human beings. In the beginning, the train was a simple thing, but because it has been refined and added to over the intervening years, it has become the pride of our times. Habit has also played a great part in its growth. Through careful observation, I saw that the people who were waiting usually chose familiar cars each time. Those who were considered leaders (or who were able to easily persuade others) seemed to be held in great regard, because then people didn't have to make their own decisions. Most passengers also felt much more comfortable when there were others on the same car, and they aided and abetted each other in their choices.

Through common usage, this "Train Of Thought" has become the universally accepted mode of transportation. All educational institutions are geared to programming their students in making the 'right' choice on the "Thought Train." The resulting systems of thought, with all their subtle nuances, are held in great esteem. These, in turn, support the whole social structure and the economic system, which explains the nervousness and outright anger that is aroused by any suggestion that there might be a better means of transportation. The constant threats to the system caused by war or natural catastrophes make a few people question the whole thing, but this rarely happens.

I have recently discovered for myself that there really is a different way of getting to where one wants to go. It is through direct perception, and the result is an instantaneous oneness with the object or situation itself, including all of its related phenomena. It eliminates having to choose anything related to "The Train Of Thought." Direct perception makes the old method of doing things seem obsolete, except as a means of continued communication with other people. I can conceive of a future state in which more and more people would use this new dimension. and thereby create a brand new society.

The new social structure would be based on *real* values in human relationships. Of course, many of the destinations of the "Thought Train" would be dropped, such as War, Prejudice, Yours, Mine, Reward, Punishment, Courage, Politics, My Country, Authority, Philosophy, and so on. There would be a complete social upheaval, since people engaged in these activities would be forced into other lines of work. It is not hard to see why the train is so ancient, nor why even the slightest effort to upset the status quo is met with resistance from all of those whose livelihood depends upon it.

Perhaps only rare individuals can step away from it from time to time.

*   *   *

Please become aware of your own "Train Of Thought" and find direct perception and now-consciousness.

Affectionately,

Al Blackburn

NOW-CONSCIOUSNESS REVIEWS:

NOW-CONSCIOUSNESS: Exploring the World Beyond Thought is a stimulating and perceptive account of Albert Blackburn's experience in transpersonal realms. The personal account of his time with Krishnamurti is especially interesting, and his treatment of the process of self-realization is — to use a word the author may regard as inappropriate — thoughtful. Blackburn writes about "the state that others have variously termed awareness, self-recollectedness, objective consciousness, *satori* in the Zen tradition and *samadhi* in Hindu literature." He offers his thoughts on perception, awareness, enlightenment, the religious life and living intelligently. He concludes the book with short aphorisms intended to express various insights he has had into "the eternal verities of life."

Echoing Krishnamurti, but on the basis of his personal realization, Blackburn shows that Truth is a pathless land and that to enter it, one must transcend thought and mental conditioning altogether, for that is the root of ego.

MIND-EXPANDER
JOHN WHITE
Author of *"Frontiers of Consciousness"*

* * *

After 73 years on this planet, the young Albert Blackburn of Ojai, California, has finally shared some of his wonderful ideas and experiences with the reading public through this very fine book. While the subject matter may appear to be difficult, the style and expression of this book are easy and flowing. I highly recommend it to everyone interested in enlightenment and self-realization.

NEWSLETTER
OTHER DIMENSIONS SERVICES
ANDY SCHNEIDER

*   *   *

We deeply appreciated your book *Now-Consciousness*. There are few people who have experienced a transformation such as yours — a transformation making them a precious source of inspiration for we disordered, violent and suffering, self-tormenting and self-torturing human beings. The readers of your book will find it a precious light for themselves and for the world.

RENÉ FOUÉRÉ
Author of *La Révolution du Réel*
KRISHNAMURTI

*   *   *

FROM OUR READERS
AND LISTENERS

I feel *NOW-CONSCIOUSNESS* is one of the most helpful books on enlightenment ever written. Bookshelves groan beneath innumerable metaphysical books which outline thought-based "systems of enlightenment." Refreshingly, Albert Blackburn's book sidesteps the sideshow of mental illusion these books encourage in their readers. It offers practical insights into sane, worry-free daily living.

J.C.
Los Gatos, CA.

* * *

I have not been as profoundly moved for a very long time as I was by your book and tapes. Your viewpoint is, for me, a beacon of light in a very dark, confusing, and chaotic world. I just feel like this: "Oh, I understand that completely. I can't see any holes in it. And it's so simple." I really feel good! Thank you!

S.A.
East Sparta, Ohio

* * *

Just a note to let you know how much I liked your book. It is a joy reading about someone who is walking in your own shoes or looking at the same mirror, and to learn about his experiences in doing it. You have offered those persons who know about Krishnamurti's teachings a unique opportunity to "see" themselves through the experiences of one who is living them and digging deeply into them.

A. C. D-R.
Santurce, Puerto Rico

* * *

Your writing appealed to me because it is presented in such a clear and lucid style. I can so easily see where some of your experiences have also happened to me, and then take them excitedly and wrap them in my own trappings and say mentally, "Yes! Yes! Yes! That is the way it happens."

S. D.
Palo Alto, CA.

* * *

The tapes arrived; thank you. I was driving home on the freeway from my office and began listening to one. In a few minutes your words helped dispel a minor state of confusion that had been besetting me. You helped me to see reality more clearly, and for that I am grateful. Thank You!

J. D.
San Rafael, CA.

* * *

Your sincerity, clarity, and passion was very inspiring to me and has helped me to see the human condition in a new, refreshing way.

H.P.
Narbeth, PA.

* * *

I've listened to your tapes, and I feel I know you. My whole being responded. I didn't realize it, but now I know I've gotten to the end of my former paths and have been wondering, what next? The wind was blowing through the trees and all the leaves were moving. For the first time I was amazed that I could take in all the movement in a glance. I didn't have to single out a single leaf, which is what I normally do.

M.C.
Eugene, OR.

* * *

I feel that our conversations were very valuable and enlightening. I learned quite a few things. It is interesting that the process of awareness was intense when I was around you. Somehow, if one is receptive, another can intensify the process in that person; I guess it is like wave resonance in physics. You see, the frequencies were the same, and in that, there's true friendship and understanding. The more I read *NOW-CON-SCIOUSNESS*, the more I discover in it. It is truly full of individual insights into all aspects of life.

K.P.
Istanbul, Turkey

* * *

Words would be useless to describe our meeting in Seattle, so I won't try. The passion to look has stayed, and questions seem to be arising daily. One of the things that happened after our meeting was I realized that whatever level of conditioning you are in at any moment, if it is perceived, really seen, that is the last step. I personally have never encountered such a person as Albert Blackburn — no, wrong — the thing that operated through that person, which in turn opened up something behind Ray.

R.B.
Victoria, B.C.

* * *

I read your book with great interest, and re-read some passages with delight. I found the chapter titles and their perceptive, one-sentence commentaries a treat, revealing as well as intriguing, urging your reader to read on. I found it an evocative way of opening up each area in your reader — me. Writing, when it is the outcome of "direct perception," carries its own validity and meaning and awakens a similar response in the reader.

D.I.S.
Newport Beach,
Australia

* * *

I'm re-reading *NOW-CONSCIOUSNESS* with much more understanding. I am in a process of leaving behind; many things no longer work for me. Your book is a guide and I begin to see the depth with which you recognize everything and are able to communicate this, simply! You have written a most important book. Like I take photographs, you are able to show something to those who take time to see, even if it is a personal understanding that makes no claims of "enlightening" others. The dimensions of the "picture" are immense and inspire creativity. Unlike my photographs, the book portrays an ongoing process that continues to be real, actual, as I approach it on different days. Thank you.

G.W.
Sonoma, CA.

FURTHER EXPLORATION INTO NOW-CONSCIOUSNESS
Discussions with Albert Blackburn

Author of
NOW - CONSCIOUSNESS:
Exploring the World Beyond Thought

Produced by:
IDYLWILD BOOKS
P. O. BOX 246, OJAI, CA 93023
(805) 646-2646
©IDYLWILD BOOKS 1985

EACH AUDIO CASSETTE:
Time: 1 Hour
Price: $6.00 each

We invite you to participate in this exciting exploration into the world beyond thought. In these tapes Albert Blackburn, with his wife Gabriele, discuss his creative and completely extemporaneous, step-by-step exploration into insight. Using the words as a mirror, the listener can be led imperceptively into an actual experiencing of what is being discussed. True listening, in which there is no judgment, evaluation or a retreat into a preconceived idea, invites holistic understanding at the level where inner transformation can occur.

#1 AN INTRODUCTION TO NOW-CONSCIOUSNESS
COVERS: A comparison between Occultism, Mysticism and Now-Consciousness. Do all paths lead to the ultimate Truth? Experiencing Reality beyond psychological time. The results of 'meditation.' What is a Religious life?

#2 DIRECT PERCEPTION
COVERS: The ending of psychological time. The possible effect of computerized living on brain development. The possibility of by-passing conditioning through direct perception.

#3 EXPERIENCING
COVERS: The fundamental difference between an experience and experiencing. How experiences are routed through the brain into the content of consciousness. Experiencing the completeness of each moment, opens the door to insight and self-discovery. With insight we can live intelligently.

#4 THE QUIET MIND
COVERS: Can the manipulation of thought, through meditation lead to a quiet mind? What is real stillness? How true stillness can come into being with no effort. The ending of the psychological 'me,' and the discovery of reality moment to moment.

NEW #5 EXPLORING THE WORLD BEYOND THOUGHT
COVERS: What is the origin of thinking? Two kinds of memory. Insight — direct action — faith. Difference between knowledge and knowing. Can one live without psychological time?

NEW #6 ENLIGHTENMENT
COVERS: The real meaning and results of Enlightenment: freedom from the known, use of a different energy, no conflict, no fear, order, integrity, understanding, faith, harmlessness, honesty and inner peace.

NEW #7 HOLISTIC UNDERSTANDING
COVERS: Four levels of understanding. Integrated understanding on all levels is the beginning of an entirely new way of living. Is suffering an intrinsic part of the evolutionary process? How to completely eliminate psychological suffering. What is spiritual alchemy?

PLEASE SEND ME:

ALL TAPES
WARRANTED
AGAINST
DEFECTS

NEW

		EACH	HOW MANY?	
#1	INTRODUCTION TO NOW-CONSCIOUSNESS	$6.00		
#2	DIRECT PERCEPTION	$6.00		
#3	EXPERIENCING	$6.00		
#4	THE QUIET MIND	$6.00		
#5	EXPLORING THE WORLD BEYOND THOUGHT	$6.00		
#6	ENLIGHTENMENT	$6.00		
#7	HOLISTIC UNDERSTANDING	$6.00		

TOTAL ORDER: _____
California Residents add 6% Sales Tax: _____
U.S. Mailing and Handling $1.00 — Others $2.00: _____
TOTAL ENCLOSED: _____

Send check or money order
payable on any U.S. Bank to:
IDYLWILD BOOKS
P.O. BOX 246
OJAI, CA 93023

ORDER TO BE SENT TO:

ᴨAME: _____

ᴅDRESS: _____

ᴛY: _____ STATE: _____ ZIP: _____

UBLISHED BY
DYLWILD BOOKS
O. BOX 246, OJAI, CA 93023
05) 646-2646

Now
Consciousness:
Exploring the World Beyond Thought
Albert Blackburn

The intimate contemporary account of one man's quest is a valuable step-by-step approach that anyone can follow on the path of self-knowledge. During an interview with J. Krishnamurti in 1944 the author underwent a radical inner transformation, a turning about at the deepest seat of consciousness. The result: Now-Consciousness, the perception of reality moment-to-moment, free of time and discrimination. This awareness leads to an inner clarity that enables the individual to objectively watch the intricacies of the thought process and explore the secrets of consciousness.

Albert Blackburn's straightforward accounting of his own experiences make this work ideal for anyone interested in the dynamics of consciousness and the psychology of transpersonal experiencing. The author disputes the necessity of a linear approach to enlightenment; instead he suggests the possibility of a vertical, instantaneous breakthrough, free of time.

N: 0-915520-64-8
paperback   /   5½ x 8½   /   176 pages
LWILD BOOKS 1983

OW CONSCIOUSNESS: Exploring the World Beyond Thought *is a stimulating and perceptive account of Albert* ackburn's/the author's experience in transpersonal realms. *The personal account of his time with Krishnamurti is especially* eresting, and his treatment of the process of self-realization is — to use a word the author may regard as appropriate — thoughtful.

John White
Author of ''Frontiers of Consciousness''

AMOUNT
PLEASE SEND ME: **NOW CONSCIOUSNESS** **HOW MANY?**_____ @ $8.95 each = _____
California Residents add 6% Sales Tax: _____
U.S. Mailing and Handling $1.00 — Others $2.00: _____
TOTAL ENCLOSED: _____

Send check or money order
payable on any U.S. Bank to:
IDYLWILD BOOKS
P.O. BOX 246
OJAI, CA 93023

ORDER TO BE SENT TO:

AME: _____

DDRESS: _____

TY: _____ STATE: _____ ZIP: _____